The Focus Group Guidebook

David L. Morgan

The Focus Group Guidebook

Focus Group Kit 1

 SAGE Publications
International Educational and Professional Publisher
Thousand Oaks London New Delhi

For information:

SAGE Publications, Inc.
2455 Teller Road
Thousand Oaks, California 91320
E-mail: order@sagepub.com

SAGE Publications Ltd.
6 Bonhill Street
London EC2A 4PU
United Kingdom

SAGE Publications India Pvt. Ltd.
M-32 Market
Greater Kailash I
New Delhi 110 048 India

Printed in the United States of America

Library of Congress Cataloging-in-Publication Data

Morgan, David L., Krueger, Richard A.
  The focus group kit.
      p.   cm.
  Includes bibliographical references and indexes.
  Contents: v. 1. The focus group guidebook/David L. Morgan.   v. 2. Planning focus groups/David L. Morgan.   v. 3. Developing questions for focus groups/Richard A. Krueger.   v. 4. Moderating focus groups/Richard A. Krueger.   v. 5. Involving community members in focus groups/Richard A. Krueger, Jean A. King.   v. 6. Analyzing and reporting focus group results/Richard A. Krueger.

  ISBN 0-7619-0760-2 (pbk.: The focus group kit: alk. paper)

  1. Focus groups. I. Title. II. Series. III. Morgan, David L. IV. Krueger, Richard A.

H61.28K778 1997
001.4'33—dc21   97-21135

ISBN 0-7619-0818-8 (v. 1 pbk.)
ISBN 0-7619-0817-X (v. 2 pbk.)
ISBN 0-7619-0819-6 (v. 3 pbk.)
ISBN 0-7619-0821-8 (v. 4 pbk.)
ISBN 0-7619-0820-X (v. 5 pbk.)
ISBN 0-7619-0816-1 (v. 6 pbk.)

This book is printed on acid-free paper.

        99   00   01   02   03   10   9   8   7   6   5   4   3

Acquiring Editor:	Marquita Flemming
Editorial Assistant:	Frances Borghi
Production Editor:	Diana E. Axelsen
Production Assistant:	Karen Wiley
Typesetter/Designer:	Janelle LeMaster
Cover Designer:	Ravi Balasuriya
Cover Illustration:	Anahid Moradkhan
Print Buyer:	Anna Chin

Table of Contents

Acknowledgments

The first acknowledgments in this volume have to go to two people who were there at every step of the way: my wife, Susan Wladaver-Morgan, and my coeditor, Dick Krueger. The readers of this kit also owe Susan a thank-you, since she has copyedited every word of every volume. Her direct contribution to this kit has been of great value to both myself and Dick. More personally, her support throughout this project has truly made it possible for me to uphold my part of the partnership. That partnership was also greatly aided by having a tremendous collaborator. From start to finish, Dick Krueger has been the steadying force that kept this project on track. His contributions to this particular volume in the kit also require recognition, since I would never have been able to meet our deadlines without his assistance. I recall well the efforts that I went through to get Dick to sign onto this project with me, and I am eternally grateful that we were able to work together.

Several other people deserve thanks for their roles throughout this project. At Portland State University, I would especially like to thank my colleagues at the Institute on Aging, Elizabeth Kutza and Margaret Neal, for all the things they have done, both large and small, that allowed me to pursue this project. At Sage Publications, I would like to thank Mitch Allen, for putting this project in motion; Marquita Flemming, for shepherding it through to completion; Ravi Balasuriya, for his inspired work on the design of these volumes; and Diana Axelsen, for all the effort that it took to get these books out the door on time. The material in this book has also benefited from several courses on focus groups that I have offered. I am especially grateful to the people who made those courses possible, including Sam Lowry and his colleagues at the Professional Development Center at Portland State; Carol Bryant and the Annual Conference on Social Marketing in Public Health at the University of South Florida; and, at the University of Michigan, Duane Alwin and Jim Lepkowski from the Survey Research Center's Summer Training Program.

A project of this scope necessarily draws from many sources. It is tempting to try and thank all of my colleagues who have aided me with the ideas in this book, but, for every name I listed, there would undoubtedly be others that I overlooked. Still, I especially want to thank John Knodel and Kerth O'Brien for the dual roles that they have played, as both friends and colleagues in focus groups. Others who made specific contributions to this volume include Al Bernstein, for his good counsel and advice; Paula Carder, who helped get things started; Adam Davis, Lourdes Gutierrez, and Amy Driscoll, who all contributed examples of focus groups in use; Alice Scannell, who was my collaborator on Volume 2; and Brian and Val Oatley, who allowed me to try and convince them that focus groups might fit into their work. Last, on the home front, I would also like to thank my son, Daniel Kang Morgan, for both his patience and his sense of humor throughout this project. Perhaps, when he sees this kit, he will finally have an answer to his question, "Dad, what it is that you *really* do?"

Introduction to the Focus Group Kit

We welcome you to this series of books on focus group interviewing. We hope that you find this series helpful. In this section we would like to tell you a bit about our past work with focus groups, the factors that led to the creation of this series, and an overview of how the book is organized.

We began our studies of focus group interviewing about the same time. Our academic backgrounds were different (David in sociology and Richard in program evaluation), and yet we were both drawn to focus group interviewing in the 1980s. We both had books published in 1988 on focus group interviewing that resulted from our research and practice with the methodology. At that time, we were unaware of one another's work and were pleased to begin a collegial relationship. Over the years, we've continued our studies independently, and occasionally our paths crossed and we had an opportunity to work together. In the last decade, we've worked together in writing articles, sharing advice on research studies, and teaching classes. We have generally found that we shared many common thoughts and concerns about focus group interviewing.

During the 1990s, we found that interest in focus groups continued, and we both prepared second editions for our 1988 books. In 1995, the staff at Sage Publications asked us to consider developing a more in-depth treatment of focus group interviewing that would allow for more detail and guide researchers beyond the basic issues. We pondered the request and thought about how the materials might be presented. We weighed a variety of options and finally developed the kit in its present form. We developed this kit in an effort to help guide both novices and experts.

In these books, the authors have occasionally chosen to use the word *we*. Although the authors share many common experiences with focus groups, our approaches can and do vary, as we hope is the case with other researchers as well. When you see the word *we* in the books of this series, it typically refers to a judgment decision by the specific author(s) of that particular volume. Much of what the authors have learned about focus groups has been acquired, absorbed, and assimilated from the experiences of others. We use *we* in circumstances where one of us personally has experienced a situation that has been verified by another researcher or when a practice or behavior has become standard accepted practice by a body of focus group moderators. The use of *I,* on the other hand, tends to refer to situations and experiences that one of us has witnessed that may not have been verified by other researchers.

In terms of content, we decided on six volumes, each representing a separate theme. The volumes include the following:

- **Volume 1:** *The Focus Group Guidebook*

This volume provides a general introduction to focus group research. The central topics are the appropriate reasons for using focus groups and what you can expect to accomplish with them. This book is intended to help those who are new to focus groups.

- **Volume 2:** *Planning Focus Groups*

This volume covers the wide range of practical tasks that need to get done in the course of a research project using focus groups. A major topic is making the basic decisions about the group's format, such as the size of the groups, their composition, and the total number of groups.

- **Volume 3:** *Developing Questions for Focus Groups*

This book describes a practical process for identifying powerful themes and then offers an easy-to-understand strategy for translating those themes into questions. This book helps make the process of developing good questions doable by outlining a process and offering lots of examples.

- **Volume 4:** *Moderating Focus Groups*

The book is an overview of critical skills needed by moderators, the various approaches that successful moderators use, and strategies for handling difficult situations. Rookie moderators will find this book to be an invaluable guide, and veteran moderators will discover tips and strategies for honing their skills.

- **Volume 5:** *Involving Community Members in Focus Groups*

This book is intended for those who want to teach others to conduct focus group interviews, particularly nonresearchers in communities. Volunteers can often gather and present results more effectively than professionals. A critical element is how the volunteers are trained and the manner in which they work together.

- **Volume 6:** *Analyzing and Reporting Focus Group Results*

Analysis of focus group data is different from analysis of data collected through other qualitative methodologies, and this presents new challenges to researchers. This book offers an overview of important principles guiding focus group research and then suggests a systematic and verifiable analysis strategy.

Early on we struggled with how these materials might be presented. In order to help you find your way around the series, we developed several strategies. First, we are providing an expanded table of contents and an overview of topics at the beginning of each chapter. These elements help the reader quickly grasp the overall picture and understand the relationship between specific sections. Second, we've attempted to make the indexes as useful as possible. Volumes 2-6 contain two indexes: an index for that volume and a series index to help you find your way around the entire kit of six books. Finally, we are using icons to identify materials of interest. These icons serve several purposes. Some icons help you locate other materials within the series that amplify a particular topic. Other icons expand on a particular point, share a story or tip, or provide background material not included in the text. We like the icons because they have allowed us to expand on certain points without interrupting the flow of the discussion. The icons have also allowed us to incorporate the wisdom of other focus group experts. We hope you find them beneficial. We've also included icons in the book to help you discover points of interest.

BACKGROUND

The **BACKGROUND** icon identifies the bigger picture and places the current discussion into a broader context.

CAUTION

The **CAUTION** icon highlights an area where you should be careful. These are especially intended to help beginners spot potholes or potential roadblocks.

CHECKLIST

The **CHECKLIST** icon identifies a list of items that are good to think about; they may or may not be in a sequence.

EXAMPLE

The **EXAMPLE** icon highlights stories and illustrations of general principles.

EXERCISE

The **EXERCISE** icon suggests something you could do to practice and improve your skills, or something you could suggest to others to help them improve their skills.

GO TO

The **GO TO** icon is a reference to a specific place in this book or one of the other volumes where you will find additional discussion of the topic.

KEY POINT

The **KEY POINT** icon identifies the most important things in each section. Readers should pay attention to these when skimming a section for the first time or reviewing it later.

TIP

The **TIP** icon highlights a good practice to follow or something that has worked successfully for us.

We hope you find this series helpful and interesting.

—Richard A. Krueger   —David L. Morgan
  St. Paul, Minnesota   *Portland, Oregon*

1

About This Book

Overview

An Introduction to Focus Groups
First Encounters With Focus Groups

This is a book for readers who are new to focus groups. Consequently, this chapter begins by introducing what focus groups are. The rest of this chapter summarizes the organization of the book and then presents two examples of what it might be like to do your first project using focus groups.

An Introduction to Focus Groups

Focus groups are group interviews. A moderator guides the interview while a small group discusses the topics that the interviewer raises. What the participants in the group say during their discussions are the essential data in focus groups. Typically, there are six to eight participants who come from similar backgrounds, and the moderator is a well-trained professional who works from a predetermined set of discussion topics. Many other variations are possible, however.

Over the past decade, many organizations have learned what focus groups are. Government agencies, nonprofit organizations, academic researchers, and public relations experts are all discovering the value of focus groups. From a practical standpoint, the real question is not what focus groups are but what you can do with them—and how to do it. The other five volumes in this kit present detailed "how to do it" information, while this book concentrates on the reasons why you might choose to do focus groups, as well as what an actual project using focus groups would involve. These twin themes—why to do focus groups and what this choice involves—begin in the second half of this chapter, which describes what it is like to do your first project using focus groups.

The broad issue of what you can do with focus groups is the central topic in Chapter 2, "Why Should You Use Focus Groups?" That chapter sets out both the strengths of focus groups and the ways they fit into a variety of purposes that organizations pursue. Chapter 3, "Focus Groups in Use: Six Case Studies," illustrates these uses by presenting descriptions of six projects that use focus groups. These cases also demonstrate the range of activities involved in actually doing research with focus groups.

Having a grasp of both why to use focus groups and what they involve paves the way for a better understanding of what focus groups are and why they are done the way they are. This is the topic of Chapter 4, "What Focus Groups Are (and Are Not)," while Chapter 5, "A Capsule History of Focus Groups," examines three traditions that have contributed to current practices in focus groups. Anything that has been around long enough to have a history will also have acquired a certain amount of mythology, and Chapter 6, "Some Myths About Focus Groups," gets at the truth behind some of the common misconceptions about focus groups.

The next two chapters consider some of the realities of doing focus groups. Making the decision about whether to do focus groups requires an understanding of the kind of results that they will produce, and this is the topic of Chapter 7, "What Do You Get From Focus Groups?" Choosing to do focus groups also requires that you have the means to do them, as discussed in Chapter 8, "Resources Required to Do Focus Groups."

Chapters 9 and 10 present the human side of focus groups. Chapter 9, "It's All About Relationships: Working Together," considers the roles in any focus group project: the sponsor (who commissions the project), the research team (who collect and analyze the data), and the participants (whose discussions provide the data). Chapter 10, "Ethical Issues," continues the theme of relationships, by examining the responsibilities that the people in these three roles have toward each other.

Finally, Chapter 11, "Checklist: Are Focus Groups Right for You?" concludes this introduction with a checklist of the issues that go into a decision to use focus groups. By the time you are done reading this book, let alone the whole kit that goes with it, you will have a solid understanding of why to do focus groups and what doing focus groups involves. In the meantime, a good way to think about whether focus groups are right for you is to review some examples of how others have used them.

EXAMPLE

Examples of Projects Using Focus Groups

A corporation wanted to ensure the success of the new employee child care center that it was building. A series of focus groups helped the company develop flexible policies that employees felt were truly "family friendly."

A federal agency wanted to learn why its national health promotion campaign was having little effect. Focus groups indicated that the message in the existing advertising was too complex; the groups considered simpler ways of expressing the same ideas.

A department's managers wanted to convince their superior that there was demand for a new program they were planning. By first holding focus groups with potential clients, they were able to develop a survey questionnaire that demonstrated a high level of interest among the company's customers.

A library wanted to help its older patrons through the changeover from a card catalog to a computerized system. Focus groups with senior library users led to a "peer counselor" plan where older volunteers demonstrated the new system throughout the months that it was introduced.

A graduate student wanted to understand the experiences of high school students with lower grade-point averages. Her thesis used focus groups to explore why these students limited their goals to "not flunking out."

A large nonprofit organization wanted to increase its activities in the African American community. Through a nationwide series of focus groups, the organization learned that it was virtually unknown in this community, despite an advertising campaign that it thought was geared to African Americans.

A state agency that was facing major cutbacks wanted to provide a job counseling program that would be of practical use to its former employees. Focus groups revealed the need for different programs among those who wanted jobs that were similar to their old ones and those who wanted to pursue new careers.

A high school-based drug prevention program was more successful at some sites than others. Follow-up focus groups comparing the more successful and less successful schools indicated the importance of connecting the program with preexisting clubs and extracurricular activities.

A health insurance plan wanted to develop the content for a multimedia program that would introduce new members to its services. The staff members conducted a series of focus groups that guided the project from its initial design phase through final product testing.

A self-help program for recent immigrants wanted to design a community center. The program hired a trainer who taught its counselors how to do focus groups among its members, eventually leading to a center that people in the community truly claimed as their own.

A major university wanted to learn the best approach to raising funds from its recent graduates. Focus groups showed that gifts were unlikely while these graduates were still paying student loans, so the university developed a low-budget campaign on the theme of "think of us when you can," with the goal of encouraging future donations.

A hospital wanted to learn why some new parents attended free childbirth classes while others did not. Focus groups showed that those who did not attend had inaccurate stereotypes about the nature of the classes, so a special brochure and publicity plan were developed to correct this.

First Encounters With Focus Groups

Focus groups don't just happen. Someone has to want to do them, and someone has to do the work. To get a realistic understanding of what is involved in the decision to do focus groups, let's consider a hypothetical scenario where a department in a large organization is getting ready to do its first project using focus groups.

Imagine that you are a manager in an organization that is about to change the way that it does business with a large percentage of your clients. Your assignment is to put together a research project that reports on how these changes will affect your clients. Although you've never used focus groups before, you've been impressed with other projects you've encountered that did use them. You're convinced that focus groups would be right for this project. Now your task is to convince your supervisor.

What kinds of things will your supervisor want to hear? First, it would probably be wise to describe exactly what focus groups are, especially if you're not sure what your supervisor may or may not know about them. More important, however, is to make a clear case about why focus groups will deliver exactly the kind of information that your organization needs.

In this case, the purpose of the project is to anticipate changes. Hearing from your clients in focus groups is going to let you know what matters to them. Are the changes going to deliver some things that they want? Will your clients experience disruptions or the loss of services that will make a major difference to them? In addition, the focus groups will help you learn about the best ways to communicate with your clients during this period of change. How can you get them the information they need in a timely fashion? How can you continue to benefit from their inputs once you have started to implement the planned changes?

These are things that your organization needs to know, and focus groups can deliver them. Still, if neither you nor your supervisor has used focus groups before, you may still face questions like, "But why focus groups? Don't we have other ways of getting this kind of information?"

In this case, it is fairly easy to make a case for the value of group discussions with your clients. Each individual client is likely to have some ideas about how these changes will make a difference, but most of them probably have not thought about these changes very deeply. Bringing a group of clients together allows them to share and compare their different ideas. They can discuss what is likely to happen and what won't, what will affect one of them but not another, and what their highest priority issues are during this period of transition. The give-and-take of group discussions among clients who share an interest in these changes should produce very useful insights into what matters most to them.

Of course, your supervisor is also going to have a series of much more pragmatic concerns. How much is this going to cost? Who is going to do this work? How long is it going to take? We address these issues elsewhere in this volume, as well as in the other books in this series. You'll need to do your homework so you can answer these questions, but, first, make sure that you can explain exactly why focus groups are the right way to accomplish what this project requires.

The best way to understand what a focus group project can accomplish is to think about the kind of report you will produce. Suppose your supervisor asks, "What are we actually going to have when we're done?" You need to be able to describe what the final report will contain. In this case, your report will describe the issues that matter most to your clients. You can summarize their priorities and offer recommendations based on their suggestions. You don't need a full technical outline of the report before you make the presentation to your supervisor, but you do need to have a good idea of what it will contain. Once again, other chapters in this book, as well as other books in this series, provide guidance on report writing.

Most important, if you use focus groups for this project, you will gain powerful insights into the feelings of the people who will be most affected by these changes. Your report will thus help those who must implement these changes understand the perspectives of the clients they will be working with. If you do it right, the report will not be just a pile of facts but a rich source of insights into the human task of implementing change.

Over the past few years, the increasing popularity of focus groups has meant that scenes like this are replayed in organiza-

Chapter 8 and *Planning Focus Groups* Have More Discussion of Timelines and Budgets

Chapter 7 and *Analyzing and Reporting Focus Group Results* Contain More Discussion of Reports on Focus Group Research

tions throughout the country. Hence, it is hardly surprising that more and more people want to acquire this skill. If this includes you, then sooner or later you will have the responsibility of carrying out your first project using focus groups. To get a feeling for what it is like to take on your first set of focus groups, consider another hypothetical scenario, where a project like the previous one is delegated to someone who will have the day-to-day responsibility for doing the work.

Imagine the first meeting to discuss your responsibilities on your new job. Your department manager hands you an assignment to do focus groups. You're in luck, however, since the person who held your job before you is available to act as your mentor. So, you immediately set up a meeting with your predecessor to find out what it takes to do a set of focus groups.

Moderating Focus Groups Discusses Moderating Focus Groups

The good news is that your mentor can help you with your number one worry: You've never moderated a focus group before. Fortunately, other focus group projects are going on elsewhere in the organization, and you'll be able to help out with those groups and watch how it is done. In addition, she has a good book for you to read.

The not so good news is that focus groups are more complicated than you had realized, and you have a lot to do in addition to moderating the groups. What do you need to do?

Planning Focus Groups Discusses Decisions About Group Composition and Recruitment Procedures

You need to make decisions about who the participants will be. Your department manager has assured you that you can recruit the participants from a list of the organization's clients, but your mentor tells you that you need to give it more thought than that. You need to think about who will really be able to talk about this topic in ways that will be useful for you to hear. Perhaps you want to compare more than one category of client to find out if different categories have different messages to share. In addition, your mentor warns you that you have to have careful recruitment procedures in place, not just to select the right participants for the groups but also to ensure that they will actually attend. You can't just assume that people will show up once you invite them. Overall, your decisions about who will be in the groups and how to recruit them will have a major influence on the success of your project.

Developing Questions for Focus Groups Discusses Writing Questions

You need to think about what kinds of questions to ask. Your department head gave you a list of topics that management wants to have covered, but the person who wrote it seems to be some upper-level bureaucrat who hasn't talked to a client in years. The topics on your list need a lot of translation just to get them to the stage where the people in your groups can understand them. Making these questions interesting to the clients is going to take even more work. It doesn't take you long to realize that your decisions about what questions to ask will have a major impact on the quality of the data that you collect.

You need to make sense of whatever data you get from the groups. Just holding successful groups doesn't mean much if you don't know how to analyze the data. Furthermore, you have to present a report that summarizes your analysis. More to the point, you need to present it in terms that your organization's managers will find useful. Somehow, you have to take what the clients say in the groups and turn this into a report that will speak to your department managers. So, right from the start, you need to concentrate on how the project will produce the end results you need.

At one level, focus groups seem simple indeed: You talk to people, and you report what they said. At another level, focus groups require a great many decisions: Whom will you talk to? How will you recruit them? What questions should you ask? How will you moderate the groups? How will you analyze the data? What will the final report look like? The point of this book is to provide you with the background that you need to think clearly about these issues, while the other volumes in this kit will supply the detailed knowledge that you need to make good decisions on all these questions.

Analyzing and Reporting Focus Group Results Discusses Analysis and Report Writing

2

Why Should You Use Focus Groups?

Listening and Learning

Focus groups are fundamentally a way of listening to people and learning from them. Focus groups create lines of communication. This is most obvious within the group itself, where there is continual communication between the moderator and the participants, as well as among the participants themselves. Just as important, however, is a larger process of communication that connects the worlds of the research team and the participants.

People who are new to focus groups too often limit their attention solely to the communication that goes on within the groups. Instead, it is important to understand that the actual groups are at the midpoint in a larger, three-part process of communication: (1) The research team members decide what they need to hear from the participants; (2) the focus groups create a conversation among the participants around these chosen topics; and (3) members of the research team summarize what they have learned from the participants.

**Listening and
Learning Should
Be the Main
Motivation**

Throughout this process, the research team's essential motivation should be a desire to listen to and learn from the participants. This is not a passive process. As a member of the research team, it is your responsibility to decide which topics you want to hear about and to focus the discussion on the things that you want to learn. At the same time, it is just as important not to be too controlling. Every group has its own dynamic, and you need to acknowledge the participants' priorities if you want to hear what they have to say. Put simply, it is *your* focus, but it is *their* group.

BACKGROUND

Group Dynamics

Anyone who has ever attended a meeting is familiar with group dynamics—the process of interaction within a set of people. Interaction is complicated enough when there are just two people doing it; bring together a group, and the possibilities are endless.

Group dynamics are about a lot more than just the personalities that happen to get mixed together in a group. If group dynamics were just about personalities, you would never be able to predict, let alone control, the interaction in groups. Things are seldom that chaotic, however, simply because we have evolved some basic strategies for managing group dynamics: Does the group have a leader? Does it have a formal agenda? The dynamics of a group that has both a leader and an agenda should be very different from a leaderless group pursuing an open discussion.

Unfortunately, the dynamics of a group don't always match its purposes. A group that is supposed to be about brainstorming may go nowhere because the leader is too controlling. In contrast, a committee charged with making a decision may get bogged down because the chair never prepares an agenda and fails to exercise any authority over the direction of the discussions.

In focus groups, it is up to the research team to create a set of group dynamics that matches the purpose of the project. You can assign different leadership styles for the moderator, and you can create an agenda through the topics in the interview guide. Depending on your purposes, the group discussion may be relatively unstructured and open-ended, with the moderator facilitating the participants' wide-ranging explorations of their thoughts and experiences. Alternatively, you may prefer to have the moderator lead a more structured discussion that provides depth and detail on precisely the questions that interest you.

It is important to remember that communication is a two-way street. Focus groups work best when what interests the research team is equally interesting to the participants in the groups. In high-quality focus groups, the questions that you ask produce lively discussions that address exactly the topics you want to hear about. When the discussions are right on target, there are even more benefits: The groups are much easier to analyze, and the final report can capture some of the excitement of the original conversations.

Although a great many things affect communication in focus groups, it is ultimately your attitude, as a member of the research team, that has the single largest influence. Imagine that this chance to communicate with the participants is a special privilege that they are granting to you. Plan for discussions that create a merger between your interests and those of the participants. Create a genuine opportunity to listen to the participants in your focus groups and to learn from them.

One of the best ways to match your interests with those of your participants is to do some role playing. Think of a focus group that you would like to do and get an image of who the participants would be. Now put yourself in the place of one of those participants.

The more concretely you do your role playing, the better it will be. For example, suppose that you, as a participant, are driving over to the focus group. Here are some questions that might be on your mind:

- *What kinds of things will you want to say about this topic?*
- *What kinds of things do you expect the other people in the group to talk about?*
- *What would you like to learn about the other people in the group?*
- *How would you like the people in the group to treat you?*
- *How would you like the moderator to treat you?*
- *How do you want to feel when the group is over?*

EXERCISE

Role Playing

Strengths of Qualitative Data

Focus groups are, above all, a qualitative research method. As such, they use guided group discussions to generate a rich understanding of participants' experiences and beliefs. Qualitative methods are an extensive field of study in their own right. For good introductions to qualitative methods, see the following:

Lofland, J., & Lofland, L. H. (1995). Analyzing social settings: A guide to qualitative observation and analysis *(3rd ed.). Belmont, CA: Wadsworth.*

Marshall, C., & Rossman, G. B. (1995). Designing qualitative research *(2nd ed.). Thousand Oaks, CA: Sage.*

Patton, M. Q. (1990). Qualitative evaluation and research methods *(2nd ed.). Thousand Oaks, CA: Sage.*

BACKGROUND

Sources on Qualitative Methods

For now, it will be enough to understand how focus groups draw on three of the fundamental strengths that are shared by all qualitative methods: (1) exploration and discovery, (2) context and depth, and (3) interpretation. For each of these three general strengths, what focus groups emphasize are the specific strengths that come from collecting qualitative data through group discussions.

Qualitative methods are especially useful for exploration and discovery. Focus groups are frequently used to learn about either topics or groups of people that are poorly understood. Because the group itself can carry on a conversation about what interests its members, it is possible for you to start a discussion even when you know very little about the topic. Focus groups are one of the few forms of research where you can learn a great deal without really knowing what questions you want to ask! Admittedly, exercising less control over the groups will lead to wide-ranging, hit-or-miss discussions—but this may be exactly what you want when your goals are exploratory and discovery oriented.

Context and depth help you understand the background behind people's thoughts and experiences. Focus groups get at these complex influences by encouraging participants to investigate the ways that they are both similar to and different from each other. Frequently, one participant will finish a careful summary of her or his thoughts, and another will respond with something like, "Yes, I hear what you're saying, but what really matters *to me* is. . . . " Through exchanges such as this, the give-and-take of the group discussion provides a context for why a participant feels one way rather than another. Hearing how the participants react to each other gives an in-depth view of the range of their experiences and opinions.

Qualitative methods also excel at interpretation—giving an understanding of why things are the way they are and how they got to be that way. In focus groups, the participants want to understand each other: How can two people who seem to be so similar have such different experiences? How can people who are outwardly very different in fact share the same beliefs? These are the kinds of encounters that make participants interested in finding out about each other, and those discussions give you the kinds of interpretive insights that you are seeking.

One way to summarize what focus groups add to each of these general strengths of qualitative methods is to say that the group discussions create a process of *sharing and comparing* among the participants. In a lively group conversation, the participants will do the work of exploration and discovery for you. Similarly, they will not only investigate issues of context and depth but will also generate their own interpretations of the topics that come up in their discussions.

Knowing these strengths is a useful first step to deciding whether focus groups are right for you. Do you need to explore poorly understood topics and discover new insights? Do you need to investigate the contexts in which your participants operate and generate in-depth data about the range of things that matter to them? Do you need to interpret how and why people think and act as they do? Any of these motivations would point you toward qualitative methods. Then, if the process of sharing and comparing that goes on in group discussions will generate the data that you need, you can be confident in your decision to use focus groups.

Projects That Use Focus Groups

What can you actually do with focus groups? Inevitably, how you use focus groups will depend on what your purposes are, and the fact that focus groups are an adaptable research method means that they can serve many purposes. An academic researcher is going to use them for different purposes than a manager in a government agency. Still, there are several basic uses for focus groups that consistently occur across many different fields.

Table 2.1 summarizes four basic uses for focus groups: Problem Identification, Planning, Implementation, and Assessment. In essence, each of these basic uses corresponds to a stage within a larger project. The various fields that make up the columns in Table 2.1 all tend to have their own versions of these four project stages. Even so, the basic uses for focus groups within any given stage will be essentially similar across fields.

Problem Identification

At this stage, the main objective is to define a goal. This early stage of a project often benefits from the processes of exploration and discovery that are among the principal strengths of qualitative methods. Focus groups are especially useful for these initial explorations because the groups can often carry on a discussion even when the research team has only minimal knowledge about the topic. When the emphasis is on discovery, the discussions are likely to be relatively unstructured and open-ended. Instead of directing the group to talk about a predetermined agenda, the research team is trying to learn what matters most to the participants themselves. For example, academic researchers use focus groups to "generate hypotheses" about new areas of investigation, while quality improvement teams listen for opportunities to

TABLE 2.1   Four Basic Uses for Focus Groups

	Academic Research	Product Marketing	Evaluation Research	Quality Improvement
Problem Identification	Generating Research Questions	Generating New Product Ideas	Needs Assessment	Identifying Opportunities
Planning	Research Design	Developing New Products	Program Development	Planning Interventions
Implementation	Data Collection	Monitoring Customer Response	Process Evaluation	Implementing Interventions
Assessment	Data Analysis	Refining Product or Marketing	Outcome Evaluation	Assessment Redesign

Case 3 in Chapter 3 Is an Example of Problem Identification

enhance the existing way of doing things. (Chapter 3, "Case 3: Assessing Community Needs" is an example of using focus groups during the problem identification stage in projects.)

Planning

At this stage, the crucial concern is finding the best way to achieve a set of goals. The planning stage in a project often continues the emphasis on exploration, but now the research team has a set of goals that guide its efforts. By pursuing this agenda in a more structured interview format, focus groups let you hear the participants' perspectives on your goals. As the participants bounce your ideas back and forth, they can provide useful suggestions about how to get where you want to go, and they can also point to potential pitfalls in your tentative plans. For example, product marketers learn how to "position" their product in relation to other products that are already on the market, while evaluation researchers find ways to design projects that are likely to produce the desired outcomes. In Chapter 3, "Case 1: Designing a First Effort at Quality Improvement," "Case 5: Generating Items for a Survey Questionnaire," and "Case 6: Anticipating Responses to a Major Change" are examples of using focus groups during the planning stage in projects.

Several Cases in Chapter 3 Illustrate the Use of Planning

Implementation

At this stage, you are often fine-tuning your original plans, rather than just waiting for success or failure to occur. During the implementation of a project, there is a need for qualitative information that provides depth and context. Discussions in focus groups can give you insights into many issues related to implementation: How are your plans working out? What can your customers or your staff tell you that will help to close a gap between expectations and actual performance? For example, evaluation researchers monitor the intervention process itself to understand the nature of programs as they are actually delivered, while product marketers determine whether advertising campaigns are getting the appropriate messages to consumers. In Chapter 3, the second set of focus groups in "Case 4: Creating an Educational Booklet" is an example of the use of focus groups during the implementation stage in projects.

Case 4 in Chapter 3 Contains an Example of Implementation

Assessment

At this stage, you are both seeking to understand what happened in this project and learning lessons that will guide your future work. Once the project is essentially complete, qualitative assessments help you interpret what happened. Discussions in focus groups can give you insights into how and why you got the outcomes that you did. Whether a project is a success or a failure, this kind of follow-up work can help you do a better job next time. For example, quality improvement teams often think of their work as a continual process where what is learned from one project feeds back into the design of future projects, and academic researchers frequently need to follow up on poorly understood results in order to determine what they should study next. Chapter 3, "Case 2: Evaluation of a Training Center," is an example of using focus groups during the assessment stage in projects.

Case 2 in Chapter 3 Is an Example of Assessment

*   *   *

Overall, there are a great many uses for focus groups. You truly are limited only by your own imagination. Still, there is no point in "overselling" focus groups. No one expects you to be using focus groups at every stage in every project. Instead, the value of focus groups is that they offer you a variety of options that can be used for many different purposes.

3

Focus Groups in Use
Six Case Studies

Overview
Case 1: Designing a First Effort at Quality Improvement
Case 2: Evaluating a Training Center
Case 3: Assessing Community Needs
Case 4: Creating an Educational Booklet
Case 5: Generating Items for a Survey Questionnaire
Case 6: Anticipating Responses to a Major Change

One of the best ways to learn about the uses for focus groups is to study successful cases. Reading about focus groups in use also gives you a sense of the reality of doing a project using focus groups, from start to finish.

What follows are six composite cases, each of which combines the features of two or more real research projects. In part, this use of composite cases protects the identity of the sponsors for some of these projects. More important, combining the features of multiple projects within each case makes it possible to demonstrate both a wider range of uses for focus groups and more approaches to doing them.

Case 1: Designing a First Effort at Quality Improvement

Goals and Purposes

The software training department in a large organization used focus groups as part of its first quality improvement initiative. The organization was about to make a major shift in its accounting software, and the department's goal was to provide classes and training that would help this change proceed as smoothly as possible.

This project also tested the utility of focus groups for the department's future quality improvement efforts. The research team hoped that the data from the focus groups would help the department's managers understand their customers by "putting a human face" on the data.

Project Size and Staff

The project consisted of three focus groups, each with six to eight participants—employees who would be using the new accounting software. Two of the department's project managers volunteered to take a week-end training class in focus groups.

Research Participants

All of the participants were (1) users of the relevant software (2) who had attended at least one of the department's software training classes. Each group lasted 1½ hours, and all were held over lunch at the employees' work sites.

Data Collection

Within the organization, this department had a poor reputation that resulted in low ratings for its mandatory classes and minimal attendance at its voluntary classes. Because the researchers were concerned that the groups might turn into "gripe sessions," they wrote a series of questions that asked the participants for advice about how to improve the upcoming software training sessions. They also emphasized the importance of being realistic, seeking advice on improvements that the training department could make within its current budget. The opening questions in the group concerned the company's software training in general, while the later questions emphasized the specific training needs of employees who would be using the new accounting software. Throughout, the moderators used a relatively structured and directive approach, keeping the conversation closely focused on the selected topics and reminding the participants of the need to make realistic suggestions for improvements.

Analysis and Reporting

Based on what they heard in the focus groups, the research team designed the specific training sessions for the accounting software changeover. The two researchers both listened to each tape and systematically listed the suggestions that the participants had generated for these training sessions. They then organized this material into a set of key themes accompanied by specific suggestions. This allowed the research team to design a new training format that was both compatible with its department's capabilities and responsive to its customers' requests. Fortunately, the new training sessions were a success. Based on this positive outcome, the new training format became a model for the department's future efforts, and the quality improvement project itself became a widely cited example of how management was "redesigning our services based on listening to our customers."

Case 2: Evaluating a Training Center

Goals and Purposes

A nonprofit training center conducted focus groups with its graduates as part of a nationally mandated accreditation review. The purpose of the focus groups was to learn how well the center's programs were preparing graduates for their experiences in the workplace.

Project Size and Staff

The project consisted of four focus groups with eight to ten participants per group. All of the groups were held in one location over a 2-week period. The project relied extensively on volunteers, based on a special course in which the students learned how to moderate the focus groups and analyze the data.

Research Participants

Two of the groups consisted of participants who had graduated within the past year, while the other two groups had graduated between two and five years ago. This division investigated whether those who had been on the job longer had different evaluations of their training. The clerical staff at the training center located the potential participants through lists of recent graduates and recruited them by telephone; all the graduates participated on a voluntary basis.

Data Collection

The groups began with an "ice-breaking" discussion of what the participants had been doing since they completed their training, followed by questions about how their training had either been of use in their work or fallen short of their needs. Another block of questions covered specific issues that were of interest to the center's staff. For example, "Was one unique, but expensive, training class really of value to the participants?" The final question asked the participants: "If you could give one piece of advice to the training center's director about how to improve the center, what would that be?" Overall, the session moved from an open-ended discussion of things that interested the participants to a more focused discussion of topics that the training center staff had selected.

Analysis and Reporting

Immediately after each group, the moderator and an assistant, who were both members of the class, reviewed the discussion on a question-by-question basis and prepared a summary of the most important issues in that group. Working with their instructor, the class then produced a list of the most important themes across the full set of groups. A comparison of the recent and the long-term graduates identified some additional weak spots where the center could improve its programs. The class presented these conclusions orally to the center's staff, and their written report was part of the center's accreditation review portfolio.

Case 3: Assessing Community Needs

Goals and Purposes

A national foundation used focus groups to explore the possible directions for a new series of programs to increase employment opportunities in the Hispanic community. Its goal was to learn about the needs of that community by listening to its members.

Project Size and Staff

The project used a total of eight focus groups that were held at four different sites nationwide. The foundation contracted with a team of university-based researchers at one site, who established ties at the other sites. The actual groups were conducted by community service workers from each of the local sites, who came to the university for a training workshop on focus groups. All the moderators were Hispanic and bilingual.

Research Participants

Two of the project sites were urban, and the research team held separate groups of men and women in these locations. The two rural sites each conducted mixed-gender groups at two different communities in each area. One interesting feature of these groups was the fact that many of the participants brought members of their families. Although the research team had planned on having eight to ten participants per group, they encouraged the additional family members to stay. Each family designated one person who took the lead role in participating in the discussion, while occasionally consulting with other family members. All of the discussions were held at local community centers and were conducted either in Spanish or a combination of Spanish and English, according to the wishes of the participants. The participants each received $25.

Data Collection

The groups began with personal accounts of the kinds of jobs that people had held and their experiences in finding work, followed by discussions of the more general issues that Hispanic workers encountered. One especially lively portion of the interview centered on reactions to a series of photographs that were designed to provoke discussion. For example, one photo showed a woman with a handful of papers leaving what appeared to be a state employment office; behind her were long lines of people. Another showed a group of Hispanic men on a street corner, talking to a man in a pickup truck who apparently had work they might do. The groups concluded within an extended exploration of what would do the most to improve employment opportunities in their community.

Analysis and Reporting

The university-based research team collected the tapes from each group and made transcripts, with translations where necessary. Comparing the different discussions showed a series of themes that occurred throughout. The strongest theme was the need to think in terms of families, rather than individual workers—a point that was clear from the start when it was families who attended the groups. There were also differences between the groups, most notably between the men and women in urban settings; these comparisons highlighted the uniquely difficult situation of single, working mothers.

What was at least as important as what the groups had to say, however, was the effect that they had on the participants. In several cases, the groups worked on the problems of their individual members, sharing not just advice but names and phone numbers for people to contact. Two of the groups passed around sign-up lists so they could continue to get together, and one even set up an appointment to hold another session on their own. The research team concluded that this showed the value of an "empowerment" approach for the future program, and the foundation began planning for community organizing as the first step in its new program.

Case 4: Creating an Educational Booklet

Goals and Purposes

A major foundation conducted focus groups to develop an educational booklet that would encourage future retirees to devote more time to volunteer activities and community service. A first set of focus groups generated material for the booklet, while a second set of focus groups sought reactions to draft versions of the booklet.

Project Size and Staff

The project consisted of eight focus groups with approximately eight participants in each group. All the groups were held in one location over a 2-month period. The research team was directed by an outside professional, working with members of the foundation's staff.

Research Participants

A review of the existing research indicated that length of retirement was one of the biggest influences on volunteering in retirement. Based on these findings, half of the groups consisted of people who had retired within the past 6 months and the other half were people who had retired between 2 and 3 years ago.

The foundation hired a professional recruiting service that located the participants through the personnel offices at several local firms that the foundation had worked with in the past. The firms were able to provide lists of people who had been retired for the appropriate lengths of time, and a member of the research firm phoned the people on these lists to locate those who were currently engaged in volunteer work. Participants each received $35.

Data Collection

The first set of focus groups, to develop the content for the booklets, moved from questions about how people made the decision to retire, through questions about their positive and negative experiences with retirement, into an extended discussion of their experiences with volunteering. A final set of questions explained the purpose of the booklet and asked the participants for their explicit suggestions about it. These discussions were relatively open-ended. The moderator's style emphasized a balance between getting answers to the project's questions and hearing from each participant in his or her own words.

In the second set of groups, after a brief get-acquainted session, each group gave feedback on various aspects of the proposed booklet. The participants reacted to different titles for the booklet and for each of its major sections, possible photos to illustrate each section, and a selection of quotations from the first groups that could accompany each section of the booklet. Each group again ended with suggestions on how to "make this be the best possible booklet about volunteering for people like you." This second set of discussions was more structured, based on a carefully planned agenda of questions about the draft of the booklet.

Analysis and Reporting

After the first set of groups, members of the foundation's staff read through a transcript of each group and located sections of the discussion that dealt with the value of volunteering, practical suggestions about ways to become involved in volunteering, and messages that would counter any negative stereotypes or other beliefs that might limit volunteering. Working with a graphic designer, the foundation staff used this information to create a mock-up version of the booklet for the second set of groups. The reactions from those later groups helped the research team in fine-tuning the design of the booklet and making final decisions about its content, including the selection of quotations and photographs.

Case 5: Generating Items for a Survey Questionnaire

Goals and Purposes

These focus groups were part of a larger research project on satisfaction with health care services. The specific purpose for the focus groups was to develop the questionnaire for a national survey on this topic.

Project Size and Staff

The project consisted of five focus groups with approximately eight participants in each group. All of the groups were held in one location over a 1-month period. The research was conducted by a university-based team, consisting of two advanced graduate students who worked under the direction of a senior professor who was also directing the larger survey.

Research Participants

There were five categories of participants in the focus groups: pregnant women, young adults with physical disabilities, older adults with recent hip-replacement surgeries, cancer survivors, and people with persistent hypertension. The goal in selecting these health conditions was to hear from people with a wide range of experiences in the health care system. One focus group was held with each category of participants. The research team located the participants through the medical records of three local hospitals that were partners in the study; participants received $25 for attending the focus group.

Data Collection

After opening the session with discussions of personal definitions of "good-quality health care" as well as positive and negative experiences with health care, the moderator explained the larger goal of conducting a survey about satisfaction with health care services. The moderator then distributed note cards and asked each person to write down three basic topics that should be included on such a survey. As the participants discussed their suggestions, an assistant transferred their ideas onto large sheets of paper from a flip pad. The participants grouped similar suggestions together on the same sheet and chose a name for each category of items. The moderator then went from page to page, asking for additional items that would go into each category. Finally, after generating as many items as possible, the moderator passed out a ballot that asked each participant to examine the lists and pick five items that "we should be sure to include on our survey." These discussions were relatively open-ended, within a carefully scripted timeline. Each of the two graduate students took turns moderating the groups while the other served as the assistant.

Analysis and Reporting

Because there was a tight timeline for conducting the national survey, the analyses related to generating questionnaire items were conducted immediately after each group. The items from the flip-chart pages, along with the ballots choosing items for the survey, served as the basic data. The two research assistants entered these data into a computer, and the senior researcher worked with the students to consolidate the lists from the different groups. Together, they created the actual survey items based on this consolidated list. There was no formal report from this project, since the survey instrument itself served as the final product.

Case 6: Anticipating Responses to a Major Change

Goals and Purposes

A state government agency conducted focus groups as part of its planning for major changes in how its frontline employees dealt with the agency's clients. By using focus groups to hear from both their clients and their employees, the agency hoped that the planned changes would improve service delivery.

Project Size and Staff

This project used a total of eight focus groups that were held in four different locations in a state. The agency used a competitive bidding process to hire a local consultant with widespread experience in focus groups. The contract included hiring a local recruitment firm to set up the groups in each of the four regions. The consultant worked with an assistant to conduct and analyze all the groups over a 6-week period.

Research Participants

There were two categories of participants: the agency's clients and its own frontline employees who dealt with these clients on a routine basis. The study began with four groups of clients, followed by four groups of employees. The groups of clients each consisted of approximately ten participants who had been using the agency's services for 2 years or more. Because the bulk of the agency's services involved local businesses that were regular clients, it was easy for the agency to supply the recruitment firm with a list of potential participants in each region. These clients agreed to participate without pay, since they were interested in having input into the planned changes in the agency's services. The groups of employees each consisted of six participants who had worked for the agency at least 1 year.

Data Collection

In the initial groups with clients, the goal was to hear about the broadest possible range of issues that they would experience as a result of the planned changes, and to hear suggestions about how to deal with these issues. The groups began with a discussion of the different ways that each participant used the agency's services. In the core set of questions, the moderator walked the participants through the process of getting service and explained the changes in a step-by-step fashion; at each step, the groups discussed how those changes might affect them and offered suggestions. At the end, the moderator asked the participants to explain which one or two changes would be most important to their own businesses.

In the second round of groups with employees, the goal was to hear detailed accounts of how the planned changes would affect the agency's staff. The discussion began with each participant describing the kinds of contacts that he or she had with clients. As in the client groups, the moderator asked a core set of questions that went through the planned changes on a step-by-step basis, with the employees describing how these changes would affect them. The moderator then presented a summary of the impacts that the planned changes would have on clients, and asked the staff to react to the clients' concerns and preferences. Finally, the groups worked together to prioritize the most important impacts of the planned changes and to generate concrete suggestions about how to address them.

Analysis and Reporting

The research team began with a systematic, question-by-question, analysis of the tape-recorded discussions in the client groups. The team summarized the key changes that clients anticipated as well as their suggestions for dealing with these changes. The researcher presented these preliminary results to the agency's management team and got their approval on a summary of these results that would be presented in the employee focus groups.

The analysis of the second round of focus groups also emphasized a question-by-question summary of employees' views, including their reactions to the summary of the results from the clients' groups. Combining these two analyses, the final report contained: a summary of the impacts that were likely to occur as a result of the changes; clients' and employees' suggestions for dealing with these changes; and a comparison of the clients' and employees' views on the planned changes.

4

What Focus Groups Are (and Are Not)

Focus groups come in all shapes and sizes. On the one hand, this variety is a considerable strength, because it gives you many options. On the other hand, it is a source of confusion, because it can be difficult to tell what is a focus group and what is not. This chapter considers three basic defining features that all focus group projects have in common: They are a research method for collecting qualitative data, they are focused efforts at data gathering, and they generate data through group discussions.

Focus Groups Are a Research Method

Focus groups are first and foremost a method for gathering research data. In any research project, you collect and analyze information so that you can answer a question that addresses a need. Although the idea that focus groups are a research method may seem completely obvious, their current popularity leads some people to call all sorts of things focus groups. Consider these questions from two students in an introductory workshop:

• The engineers in our company hold weekly meetings that they call focus groups. Everyone reports on the status of their projects, and they make decisions about what the priorities are for the following week. We tape record those groups and put the transcripts out on the network for people to review. Are those focus groups?

• The director of our unit periodically holds these things that she calls focus groups. She sits up at the front of the room and asks us questions. She probably thinks she is getting great information, but the truth is that no one would dream of saying anything that she didn't want to hear. Then, she finishes up by telling us what she wants us to do. Would you say those are focus groups?

The obvious problem with both of these examples is that neither one involves research. Granted, information is being gathered and exchanged, but these groups are not systematically answering a question. Instead, the first case is more like an ongoing progress report, while the second is a thinly disguised attempt to control employees.

To understand how focus groups function as a research method, it is useful to compare them with what is probably the best-known contemporary research method: the survey questionnaire. Both surveys and focus groups are techniques for gathering information from people. In both cases, the researchers select the interview topics, and the survey respondents or focus group participants provide the data. Once the data are collected, it is up to the research team to analyze this information and relate the results to the original research questions.

The differences between these methods are also instructive, however. In surveys, there are well-defined sampling procedures that rely on statistical formulas. In focus groups, the research team uses its judgment to select "purposive samples" of participants who meet the needs of a particular project. Surveys use a fixed set of questions, and every respondent is asked exactly the same questions, with exactly the same set of predetermined response options. Focus groups allow considerable flexibility in how questions are asked from group to group; in addition, the nature of the responses is inherently up to the participants themselves. When it comes to analysis, surveys lend themselves to numerical summaries that reduce the data to tables and figures. The analysis of focus groups, however, involves a more subjective process of listening to and making sense of what was said in the groups.

The basic point here is that focus groups and surveys use very different approaches in meeting the more general goal of gathering information. In order to select a method that will suit your purposes, you need to understand what any given method, including focus groups, can and cannot do.

One consistent difference between focus groups and surveys is the fact that, at every step of the way, focus groups are more open-ended and less predetermined than surveys. The fact that focus groups are not nearly as standardized as surveys is undoubtedly one source of the confusion over what a focus group is and what it is not. The reason for this lack of standardization was noted in Chapter 2. Unlike surveys, focus groups rely on the strengths of qualitative methods, including exploration and discovery, understanding things in depth and in context, and interpreting why things are the way they are and how they got that way. To serve these purposes, focus groups and other qualitative methods require a great deal of openness and flexibility.

Chapter 2 Discusses the Strengths of Qualitative Research Methods

Comparing focus groups with surveys naturally raises the question of how focus groups compare with other qualitative methods, such as participant observation and individual, or "one-on-one," interviewing. Hence, the next two sections expand on the fundamental characteristics of focus groups in ways that also compare focus groups with, first, participant observation and, then, individual interviews.

Focus Groups Are Focused

Focus groups are created by a research team for a well-defined purpose. Even when the groups are primarily exploratory, they are still focused on the research team's interests. In essence, focus groups are special occasions devoted to gathering data on specific topics. A fair amount of planning goes into focus groups. The research team determines not only what the questions will be but also who will attend the group. Rather than attempting to observe behavior as it naturally occurs, focus groups create concentrated conversations that might never occur in the "real world."

This reliance on a researcher-created situation is very different from participant observation, which concentrates on understanding naturally occurring behavior. Participant observation requires the researcher to become immersed in some ongoing setting. By both observing and participating in that setting, the researcher learns what life is like there. When it comes to collecting data, the participant observer has to take whatever comes. Sometimes, this produces insights that the researcher could never have anticipated. Other times, it produces tedious encounters with topics that are either already well-known or hopelessly off target.

In contrast, focus groups produce large amounts of concentrated data in a short period of time. This more efficient method of data collection has its costs, however, since focus groups do not provide the richly textured view of life that comes from participant observation. This trade-off between researcher-targeted specificity and naturally occurring richness is hardly unique to focus groups—all interviews are essentially situations that researchers create for the purpose of hearing about the topics that interest them.

Whether the differences between focus groups and participant observation amount to an advantage or a disadvantage depends upon the kind of data that you need. When you need to know how things operate within their natural contexts, then participant observation has many advantages over focus groups. The same is true when you need to observe processes while they actually occur. If, however, you need to gather substantial amounts of carefully targeted data within a relatively short period, then focus groups are more appropriate.

Focus Groups Use Group Discussions

What distinguishes focus groups from any other form of interview is the use of group discussions to generate the data. During the discussions in a focus group, you learn a great deal about the range of experiences and opinions in the group. You do not, however, learn all that much about each specific individual. For example, if a focus group consists of six people discussing some five questions for a total of 90 minutes, each participant will be speaking for 3 minutes per question, on average. Although a great deal of sharing and comparing gets done during a group discussion, the amount of data that you obtain from each individual participant will necessarily be limited.

The most obvious difference between individual and group interviews is the amount of information that they provide about each interviewee. Even the briefest individual interview generates far more data about that person than you would get from an equivalent group interview. Some one-on-one interviews generate extensive amounts of data; for example, a complete oral history may take weeks or even months of interviewing.

This difference in the volume of data also translates into differences in timelines. Consider a comparison between 20 individual interviews and three focus groups of six to eight participants. Even with relatively brief individual interviews, collecting and analyzing data from 20 people has a very different timeline from working with three focus groups. Although the 20 individual interviews would generate far more data than the three focus groups, they would be unlikely to give you six times as much information—due in large measure to the overlap from one interview to the next.

Although the differences between individual and group interviews might at first seem slight, it should be clear by now that these two methods actually generate very different kinds of data. Here are two questions to help you decide between them:

- Is the additional information that you get in individual interviews a source of valuable insights or a waste of time?
- Are the group discussions from focus groups a more efficient way to get at what you want or a serious loss of information about the individual participants?

The answers to these questions depend on how much you need to hear detailed personal accounts about the unique experiences of particular people. Individual interviews excel at providing that kind of data. Focus groups sacrifice details about individuals in favor of engaging the participants in active comparisons of their opinions and experiences.

A Few Things That Are Not Focus Groups

Having considered what focus groups are, it is also important to understand what they are not. The popularity of focus groups has led to a certain amount of abuse of the term, so that any number of things get called focus groups even though they fall outside of the current definition.

There are three basic reasons why something might be called a focus group even if it is not. First, it might not be a research effort to gather qualitative data. Too often, groups with other intentions get called focus groups. Second, it might not be focused. A surprising number of slipshod efforts to talk with groups of people somehow get labeled focus groups. Finally, it might not involve group discussion. Just gathering people together does not guarantee that a meaningful discussion will occur.

Groups That Do Not Involve Research. By far the most common abuse of the label *focus groups* comes from applying it to things other than research. Focus group are currently very popular. Because so many people are interested in focus groups, this label gets applied to all kinds of other group work. Sometimes, mislabeling is done out of sheer ignorance about what focus groups really are. At other times, it is an attempt to tag onto the coattails of true focus groups. Either way, the result is confusion between the use of group discussion to gather qualitative data and the myriad other uses that human beings have found for groups.

It thus bears repeating that focus groups are a research technique for gathering qualitative data. They most decidedly are *not*:

Sales attempts or educational seminars

Ongoing committees

Decision-making groups or consensus-building sessions

Support groups or therapy sessions

Any of these activities and many more can be done in groups, but those groups are all something other than focus groups. True, some of these things may occur as a side effect of focus groups—participants may feel educated or supported, and they may be excited by the consensus they have reached. Still, these outcomes should be incidental benefits from a process that is primarily about gathering information.

Groups That Are Not Focused. Focus groups require careful planning to invite the right participants and ask the right questions. They also require a thoughtful approach with regard to moderating style and group dynamics. Some things that get called focus groups lack this careful preparation. For example, public forums and open meetings may be good ways to hear a wide range of opinions, but they are too unstructured to be focus groups. Similarly, a researcher might learn a great deal from the observation of a naturally occurring group, but if the researcher does not take a role in directing the discussion, this is not a focus group.

Even when a research team intends to hold a true group interview, the effort may fail due to a lack of focus. It is ordinarily the moderator's responsibility to keep the group focused, but untrained or inept moderators may not be able to maintain a coherent discussion. Given the poor quality of the data from those discussions, there is no point in calling them focus groups. Ultimately, whether a group is focused or not is a characteristic of the discussion itself, not the mere presence of a moderator.

Groups That Do Not Engage in Discussions. In focus groups, the discussions are the data. Other types of groups bring people together to collect data through something other than discussions. Among the social science methods for group data collection are *nominal groups,* which bring together the separate ideas of participants, and *Delphi groups,* which assemble the thoughts of expert panels (for more information on these techniques, see Stewart & Shamdasani, 1990).

Unfortunately, not everyone makes such careful distinctions between focus groups and other forms of group data collection. For example, during the 1996 presidential election, *Newsweek* ran a picture of a "focus group" that consisted of 30 people using handheld electronic "meters" to record their responses. Even if a group discussion supplemented the numerical data from these meters, a group this large would certainly be too unfocused to meet the previous criterion.

The idea of counting responses using electronic meters is an advanced form of an all-too-common abuse of focus groups: "counting heads" rather than relying on group discussions for the data. It is hard to understand why one would want to assemble a group of people in order to tally their individual responses. Still, some people who claim to be holding focus groups actually spend most of the time having people fill out ballots or hold up their hands. On occasion, asking for a show of hands can be a good way to gauge the group's response to a topic, and it can stimulate further discussion. Such head counting should not, however, be the primary means of data gathering.

Some researchers actually seem to fear group discussion. One research team sent out instructions for conducting a "focus group" where the moderator was supposed to go around the table and make sure that each person gave a separate response to each question in the interview guide. Otherwise, the instructions explained, having people respond to each other would damage "the scientific validity of the data." Group interviews that insist on separate responses are sometimes referred to as "serial interviews." A focus group that does not generate a lively discussion may end up being more like a serial interview, and this can still produce useful data. The real problem arises when the research team purposely tries to block the group discussion that is essential to focus groups.

Overall, the definition of focus groups has very elastic boundaries. Still, there are limits to what one can call a focus group. Fundamentally, there must be an effort to gather research data through a focused group discussion. Within those broad boundaries, a great many things are possible.

5

A Capsule History of Focus Groups

The history of focus groups can be divided into three periods. The earliest work was carried out primarily by social scientists in both academic and applied settings. Then, from World War II through the 1970s, focus groups were used almost exclusively in marketing research. Most recently, focus groups have come into common usage across a number of fields.

The goal of this chapter is to consider the contributions that these different fields have made to the development of focus groups. As such, it is an appreciation of different traditions, rather than a detailed history of focus groups (for more information on this history, see Krueger, 1994, and Morgan, 1997).

Social Science Origins

Social scientists have used various forms of group interviews since at least the 1920s. During this early period, people such as Emory Bogardus and Walter Thurstone used various types of group interviews for various purposes, including the development of survey instruments—foreshadowing one of the popular current uses for focus groups. Such efforts had little impact, however, until the groundbreaking work by Robert Merton and Paul Lazarsfeld.

Merton and Lazarsfeld were colleagues in the Department of Sociology at Columbia University (although Lazarsfeld was equally well-known as a political scientist). Their collaboration in developing group interviews began just before World War II and achieved full flower during the war itself. Like many social scientists, Merton and Lazarsfeld contributed to the war effort, using focus groups to develop propaganda materials for the home front, create training manuals for the troops, and investigate basic social issues, such as racial segregation in the armed forces.

BACKGROUND

Merton and Lazarsfeld's First Focus Groups

The initial collaboration on focus groups between Merton and Lazarsfeld is documented quite well, thanks to Merton's account (Merton et al., 1990). In fact, when the two men first met, Lazarsfeld had already been experimenting with group interviews as a way of judging audience responses following live radio broadcasts. Shortly after Merton joined the faculty at Columbia University, Lazarsfeld invited him to observe one of these groups. During the group, Merton grew dissatisfied with the way that the interviewer asked leading questions, and he suggested to Lazarsfeld that letting the participants speak more for themselves would produce better data. Lazarsfeld immediately took Merton up on his suggestion by having him moderate the group that followed the next program! Thus began the partnership that created focus groups as we know them today.

After the war, Merton and two of his students, Patricia Kendall and Marjorie Fiske, wrote a book describing focus groups, which has been reprinted several times (Merton, Fiske, & Kendall, 1990). Beginning as a 1946 article by Merton and Kendall in the *American Journal of Sociology*, their work, *The Focused Interview*, appeared as a full-fledged book in 1956. The title of this volume eventually gave the name "focus groups" to group interviews, even though it dealt equally with both individual and group versions of semistructured, qualitative interviews. Although Merton and his coauthors preferred not to make a major distinction between group and individual interviews, they did give a detailed description of the issues that arose in conducting interviews with groups. The importance of this early work is most evident in the similarity between current practices and that original description of group interviews, nearly 50 years ago. Yet, throughout most of those years, focus groups were almost unknown within the social sciences.

The Move to Marketing

From roughly 1950 to 1980, focus groups were seldom found outside of marketing research. In part, social scientists created this shift by turning their attention to other methods. Starting in the 1950s, sociologists and political scientists, such as Merton and Lazarsfeld, were increasingly drawn to survey research, especially large-scale, national surveys. The move to marketing research was also driven, however, by the uses that marketers themselves created for focus groups.

Lazarsfeld's earliest use of group interviews—gauging consumers' responses to radio programs—was the direct connection between marketing research and focus groups. Lazarsfeld himself was quite interested in marketing research, and he often used marketing projects to supplement the other sources of funding that kept his various research enterprises afloat. Based on his successes with focus groups, others in the marketing community became interested. Even so, it was not sociologists or political scientists who had the most influence on how marketing researchers used focus groups.

Marketing researchers in this era frequently referred to focus groups as "group depth interviews" (Goldman & McDonald, 1987). The emphasis on depth corresponded to an effort to uncover consumers' psychological motivations. Hence, many prominent practitioners of marketing research in this period were clinical psychologists, trained in probing the unconscious sources of behavior.

One well-known example of the group depth interview involved the sale of boxed cake mixes. This product initially received a poor reception in the marketplace, and focus groups showed that women felt they should put more effort into making something as special as a cake for their families. These focus groups led to the successful strategy of requiring the cook to use an egg in the preparation of a boxed cake mix, replacing the original practice of simply including a powdered egg in the mix. Apparently, the act of breaking an egg into the mix, rather than merely adding water, created more of the feeling of making a cake "from scratch."

EXAMPLE

Boxed Cake Mixes

Techniques involving focus groups were not taught in psychology departments, however, nor were they typically taught in schools of business administration. Instead, an eclectic mix of focus group practitioners brought their varied backgrounds to marketing firms, where they received on-the-job training in conducting focus groups. Someone with a background in psychology might have an edge in getting hired to do focus group research in marketing, but no formal training was required.

One important legacy of the marketing research approach to focus groups was the development of professional facilities for holding groups and professional services for recruiting group participants. Today, professional focus group facilities typically offer not just a comfortable room for the group itself but also a viewing room for observers (often the sponsor who is paying for the project), taping facilities for recording the group, and catering services for both the participants and observers. The same firms that rent out these facilities often provide recruitment services as well. In some cases, these recruitment services work from existing lists of potential participants—usually people who have been in their previous groups. In other cases, they have telephone recruiting rooms where employees call potential participants.

Planning Focus Groups Describes Professional Facilities and Recruiting Services

The availability of these facilities and recruiting services has undoubtedly contributed to the rising number of independent consultants who conduct focus group projects on a contract basis. The ability to rent a focus group facility on an as-needed basis eliminates one of the major expenses in doing this work, and the ability to hire recruitment services reduces the need to employ additional staff. At the extreme, a solo consultant with an answering machine and an ad in the Yellow Pages can pursue a career in focus groups.

In many ways, the developments that marketing researchers made in the focus group technique were not nearly as influential as they could have been. Because they were largely commercial practitioners, rather than scholars, very few of these researchers published descriptions of their methods. Similarly, because focus groups were not part of the curriculum in business schools, they received very little attention in marketing textbooks. All of this changed in the late 1980s when three books on marketing research uses of focus groups appeared, but, by then, these publications were only one part of a general upsurge of interest in focus groups.

A Widespread Research Method

EXAMPLE

Contraception in Mexico

Applied social research was the primary vehicle that spread focus groups beyond the world of product marketing. In particular, focus groups were involved in some of the earliest efforts at "social marketing," which is the attempt to use marketing techniques for public health and other prosocial purposes. In 1981, Evelyn Folch-Lyon and her colleagues published a set of articles describing their efforts to promote the use of contraceptives in Mexico. Working with a marketer, William Novelli, they used a combination of focus groups and surveys to explore the knowledge, attitudes, and practices about contraception among several segments of the Mexican population. Many of the features of this project have been repeated in subsequent work, including the use of focus groups to compare different "segments"—in this case, rural and urban settings, more educated and less educated participants, and so on.

Issues related to sexual behavior were also central to another early applied research project, this time involving the AIDS epidemic. Working under a contract with the Centers for Disease Control (CDC), Jill Joseph, MD, and her colleagues used focus groups to develop the content for a questionnaire that surveyed gay and bisexual men in response to the emerging epidemic. Because both the CDC and the research team needed to learn more about sexual practices in this community, they used focus groups as an exploratory technique prior to writing their survey. In particular, they relied on these discussions to generate the wordings for survey items that would be meaningful to a population that had seldom been systematically surveyed.

EXAMPLE

Developing a Survey on AIDS

These remain among the better known studies within what was, in retrospect, a rapidly growing field. Focus groups have become an increasingly popular tool in applied social research, especially in the health field. An important legacy of the early use of focus groups on population control has been their popularity throughout the economically developing world. One of the more notable research programs in this arena has been the demographic work of John Knodel in Thailand and elsewhere. At various times, Knodel and his coworkers have used focus groups to study declines in fertility following modernization, parents' educational preferences for young boys and young girls, attitudes toward prostitution, and, in one especially ambitious study, the support that adult children in five Asian countries supplied to their aging parents (Knodel, 1995).

Closer to home, evaluation researchers in the United States began to make extensive use of focus groups. Building on Michael Patton's work in qualitative evaluation, one of his colleagues, Richard Krueger, explored the uses of focus groups at all stages within the evaluation cycle. In 1988, the first edition of Krueger's text, *Focus Groups: A Practical Guide for Applied Research,* provided an important systematic statement on why and how to do focus groups. This approach became quite popular among public agencies and nonprofit organizations that wanted to increase the effectiveness of their programs. It also became an important element of quality-improvement initiatives in these agencies and organizations, as they began the process of listening to their customers.

By this time, academic social scientists were rediscovering focus groups. In 1984, David Morgan and Margaret Spanish published one of the first articles that called attention to focus groups as a method for qualitative research in the social sciences. In 1988—the same year that Krueger introduced focus groups to applied researchers—the first edition of Morgan's *Focus Groups as Qualitative Research* promoted their use among academic researchers. Both the Krueger (1994) and Morgan (1997) volumes are now in second editions. The combined success of this emphasis on applied and academic research is evident in Morgan's (1996) estimate that social science journals are currently publishing over 100 articles per year using focus groups.

Marketing research has certainly not ignored focus groups during this period. Indeed, focus groups have played a central role in one of marketing's most controversial products—political candidates. If focus groups help influence consumers' preferences for cake mix, or their purchase of automobiles, then why not their selection of politicians?

EXAMPLE

Focus Groups and Negative Advertising

The use of focus groups in political campaigns received close examination after they were involved in the development of the so-called Willie Horton ad during the 1988 Bush-Dukakis presidential race. Political consultants affiliated with the Bush campaign used a series of focus groups to gauge reactions to a number of Dukakis's actions as governor of Massachusetts. The participants generated their most intense reaction when they learned that Dukakis was involved in paroling a convicted murder who then killed again. The ad that was based on these groups, showing a series of convicts passing through a turnstile, continues to be a major turning point in the debate over "negative campaigns."

On a less controversial note, marketing research in academic settings has shown a greater interest in focus groups. Classes in marketing research now routinely teach about them, and they receive thorough coverage in most marketing texts. In part, this shift reflects the fact that businesses are now purchasing over $1 billion worth of focus group research per year. In addition, marketing's increased recognition of focus groups has been part of a rising appreciation of qualitative research in that field, as well as in many others.

The Future of Focus Groups

Just as marketing researchers have increased their interest in qualitative research, qualitative evaluation has made similar advances in the past two decades, and academic research also exhibits more balance between qualitative and quantitative methods. Focus groups have unquestionably benefited from this growing interest in qualitative methods, and they may even have contributed to it.

It would be foolish to assume that any rapidly rising curve will continue its unchecked growth. Still, the widespread use of focus groups since 1980 shows no sign of stopping. Given all this interest in focus groups, it becomes even more important to ensure that this work is done with integrity. The gathering of poor-quality data is one thing that would surely slow the growth of focus groups. It is thus the goal of this volume, as well as this kit as a whole, to protect the future of focus groups by promoting the highest standards possible.

6

Some Myths About Focus Groups

Overview
Focus Groups Are Low-Cost and Quick
Focus Groups Require Professional Moderators
Focus Groups Require Special Facilities
Focus Groups Must Consist of Strangers
Focus Groups Will Not Work for Sensitive Topics
Focus Groups Produce Conformity
Focus Groups Must Be Validated by Other Methods
Focus Groups Tell You How People Will Behave
Some Beliefs That Should Be Encouraged

L ike most research methods, focus groups have acquired a certain amount of mythology. Some of these myths come from assumptions that were useful at one time but now need to be updated. Others come from ideas that work well in specific circumstances but are erroneous when applied to focus groups in general. Thinking through the real issues behind many of these myths will help you make better decisions about when to use focus groups and why. In the same spirit of promoting better decision making, this chapter concludes with a brief look at some beliefs that we do encourage.

Focus Groups Are Low-Cost and Quick

One of the most common myths about focus groups is that they are cheap and quick. Yes, on occasion, focus groups can be done quite cheaply—if you are willing to donate lots of your own time and energy. Similarly, they can be done quickly—if you have either a great deal of expertise or a large budget. These situations are, however, the exception rather than the rule.

If you begin with the mistaken assumption that focus groups are easy to do on a small budget and a tight timeline, you are asking for trouble. It is an entirely different matter if you begin with the realization that doing focus groups either cheaply or quickly takes careful planning and special resources. Richard Krueger provides the following example of focus groups that were done at a minimum cost.

EXAMPLE

The Cheapest Focus Group

Two retired faculty members at the university asked for information about focus group research. I asked them to stop over and talk. We visited for a couple of hours, and I gave them a number of handouts, some training materials, and a few suggestions. We had a delightful conversation, and I frankly thought that it was purely a social visit. I was surprised when they called again three months later and asked if I wanted to see their focus group report for their church. The report was impressive; in fact, it would have ranked well against studies conducted by professional moderators. I asked, "How much did this study cost?" They smiled and said, "Well, it took four big pots of coffee and four dozen cookies." All of their time was donated. This was the cheapest focus group study I had ever heard of.

—Richard Krueger

Perhaps the idea that focus groups are low-cost and quick came about through the comparison with other research methods. Chapter 4 provided brief comparisons between survey research and focus groups, and it is often the case that a set of focus groups will be less expensive and quicker than a full-scale survey. For example, if a decent survey costs $50,000 and takes 6 months, then a $20,000 set of focus groups that takes 6 weeks can be quite attractive. This is seldom a fair comparison, however, since the two methods produce such different kinds of data.

In comparison with other qualitative methods, focus groups are often more expensive than either participant observation or individual interviews, due to more expensive recruiting costs. Where focus groups may have an advantage over other qualitative methods is in terms of the speed of data collection, since a set of group interviews typically takes less time than a set of individual interviews or observations.

Prior experience is the best guide to determining whether focus groups can be done cheaply or quickly. If you already know how to do focus groups well, then you can probably figure out how to cut the budget and tighten the timeline. In particular, experienced focus group researchers know the difference between the 2 hours that it takes to conduct a group and the longer period that it takes to do the full project. If you are still in the process of gaining this experience, pay careful attention to Chapter 8 and *Planning Focus Groups* for advice on the amount of time that goes into planning and analysis, since these two areas are potentially costly and time-consuming.

Chapter 8 and *Planning Focus Groups* Emphasize the Time That Goes Into Planning and Analysis

Focus Groups Require Professional Moderators

It is tempting to speculate that this myth was created and perpetuated by professional moderators to protect the fees that they charge. The idea that these professionals have valuable expertise is not a myth. The myth is that focus groups cannot be done *without* this expensive expertise.

To decide whether you truly need a professional moderator, it is important to think about all the roles that this person might play on your project. On occasion, the moderator does little more than conduct the groups; more commonly, however, this person is actively engaged in many more aspects of the project. In the beginning of the project, it is often the moderator who writes the interview questions. At the end of the project, the same person who moderated the groups often analyzes the data and writes the report. Ask yourself, Can your own research team do it all—from the initial design of the project, through the groups themselves, to the writing of the final report? If not, then you may well want to rely on the services of a professional.

A slightly different version of this myth implies that professional moderators are necessary in order to produce the best data. In other words, you might be able to use someone from your own organization as the moderator, but you will pay a price in terms of data quality. This makes it sound as if there is a direct trade-off where the quality of the data depends on the experience of the moderator. Like many myths, this one has an element of truth in it. Yet, it is not the amount of experience itself that matters most. Instead, the moderator's experience will be most valuable when it is directly relevant to the topics and participants in your actual project.

Sometimes, a less experienced moderator who has more contact with the issues will produce better data than a professional moderator who has never worked in your area. This is especially true when you are working with distinctive ethnic, linguistic, and cultural groups. Someone who either comes from that community or is familiar with it may be by far the best choice for a moderator. Often, the crucial background for a project comes from knowledge of the research topic or familiarity with the participants, not from professional training in focus groups.

Once we dispose of the myth that professionals are essential to focus groups, it is just as important that we not create the alternative myth that "anyone can do focus groups." Make no mistake—becoming an expert moderator takes work. Think about other skills that you have tried to acquire. Perhaps you wanted to learn how to juggle, or how to make stained glass, or how to cook French cuisine. Admittedly, each of these things will be easier for some people than for others, but—like good moderating—all of these skills require a real investment of effort.

All in all, the best moderator is not the one with the most experience at moderating but the one who can help you learn the most from the participants that you need to listen to. In some cases, this might take an expert moderator. In other cases, an outside professional might actually detract from what your own research team is able to do best.

Focus Groups Require Special Facilities

Actually, focus groups can be done in any number of places. Notions about the "best" place to do focus groups—or even the most "typical" place to do them—vary widely. For example, marketing researchers in the United States often use professional facilities so the project sponsor can observe the groups and then debrief with the moderator afterward. In Britain, however, a large proportion of all focus groups are done in the living rooms of private homes.

It thus seems that the facility one considers "best" for focus groups depends upon the traditions researchers are familiar with. For applied researchers in the public sector, it is traditional to hold focus groups in places such as meeting rooms at restaurants, school libraries, and conference or seminar rooms of all sorts. If a researcher is working for a nonprofit organization or a government agency, it might be a scandalous waste of money to rent a professional facility with an observation room. Yet, if that same researcher is doing a marketing project for a business firm, it might be equally scandalous not to use a professional facility.

Aside from the importance of tradition, this also points to the robustness of focus groups. If the participants are truly interested in the discussion, it probably matters little where the group is held. The obvious answer is to think about both the needs of the research team and the comfort of the participants, and then to choose your location accordingly.

Planning Focus Groups Discusses Choosing a Location

Focus Groups Must Consist of Strangers

This is a good example of an approach that is useful for some purposes and irrelevant for many others. Once again, the use of strangers is a tradition that got its start in marketing research, where it is often the best option. Think about a group of consumers discussing a product they interact with largely out of habit, such as bar soap or breakfast cereal. Even expensive items, such as the cars they drive, become part of people's routines. Yet, if they have to explain to a group of strangers what they eat for breakfast and why, then they must provide quite a lot of information that a person would take for granted in describing the same thing to a family member or friend. So, holding a discussion among strangers is useful when you want the participants to think about and talk about their taken-for-granted assumptions.

The goal of hearing about taken-for-granted assumptions is hardly limited to marketing research, so there are many situations where it makes sense to recruit groups of strangers. It is just as true, however, that there are many other situations where it would be either impossible or undesirable to recruit strangers. In fact, many focus groups in organizational and community settings are composed of people who know each other. Sometimes, this is unavoidable, such as when you want to hear from a group of coworkers. Other times, it is highly desirable, such as when you want to re-create some of the context that you are trying to understand.

Admittedly, there are important differences between doing focus groups with strangers versus acquaintances, but this simply means that you have to adapt the method according to the circumstances.

Focus Groups Will Not Work for Sensitive Topics

The reality is that researchers with considerable experience in the use of focus groups think of them as a very useful tool for investigating sensitive topics. Hence, focus groups are commonly used in research projects related to sexual behavior, substance abuse, and stressful life events.

This myth seems to be based on common sense conceptions of what people are willing to discuss in groups. The obvious idea is that people will not talk about private matters or taboo topics in front of others. This might be true in a conversation around the dinner table or at a meeting of an ongoing community organization, but focus groups are an unusual group setting. Consider the fact that an interviewer is encouraging everyone in the group to share thoughts and experiences about a topic that interests all of them. Furthermore, there may be few consequences to whatever the participants say—especially if they are talking with strangers they will never meet again. This kind of group actually encourages people to say things they would ordinarily keep private.

The idea that focus groups will not work with sensitive topics can be a very dangerous myth. Too often, novice researchers start with the assumption that they have to work hard to draw out personal information, and then they are shocked by the kinds of personal and emotional revelations that can occur in focus groups. Such disclosures can create serious ethical problems. Although participants may experience a dizzying sense of excitement while disclosing their deepest secrets during a group catharsis, they are likely to be distressed about what they have revealed when they wake up the next day.

Chapter 10 Discusses Ethical Issues and Sensitive Topics

Researchers who work with sensitive topics must make plans both to encourage appropriate self-disclosures and to discourage disclosures that go beyond the legitimate aims of the research. Chapter 10, on ethics, discusses these issues in some detail.

Focus Groups Produce Conformity

It would be more accurate to say that focus groups *can* produce conformity. Consequently, you need to concentrate on the goal of generating a wide-ranging discussion that encourages people to share different points of view. Both the way you write your questions and the way you moderate the groups provide several options for minimizing conformity problems.

It is interesting to speculate that this myth may have arisen through a confusion between focus groups and other kinds of groups. In particular, there is a rich social psychological tradition of studying group decision making, where conformity is a central issue. Yet, decision-making groups seldom use either the trained moderators or well-developed questioning routes that are so common in focus groups. Furthermore, any pressure for the group to make a decision or reach a consensus is foreign to the climate in focus groups. Instead, focus groups emphasize the goal of finding out as much as possible about participants' experiences and feelings on a given topic. When the participants realize that the research team is genuinely interested in learning about the full range of their experiences and feelings, then conformity becomes less of a problem.

Developing Questions for Focus Groups and *Moderating Focus Groups* Discuss Ways to Minimize Conformity

Focus Groups Must Be Validated by Other Methods

This is part of a general myth that relegates all qualitative methods to a preliminary, exploratory role that prepares the way for "real research." Certainly, focus groups *can* serve a useful role as a first stage in developing all kinds of projects, including survey questionnaires and experimental interventions. This does not mean, however, that they *must* be limited to that role.

Attacking the myth that focus groups must be backed up by other methods is not the same as attacking judicious combinations of qualitative and quantitative methods. Just as there are many situations where focus groups alone are more than adequate, there are also many situations where a combination of methods will yield more useful data than any one method alone. In particular, there is nothing wrong with the already classic use of focus groups in the early stages of other research projects, so long as this does not lead to the mistaken conclusion that focus groups are useful only for preliminary exploration.

There are at least two sources for this myth. First, because focus groups are quite frequently used to develop surveys or interventions, some people have never encountered any other use for focus groups. Even supposedly well-informed researchers are sometimes surprised to learn that focus groups can be used as the sole source of data in a project.

Earlier practices in marketing research are another source of this myth. In marketing, it often makes sense to begin with focus groups as an exploratory technique and then follow up with surveys to check the focus group results in a larger sample. This is necessary because assessing the potential sales for a product often requires the generalizability that is a particular strength of surveys. If your goals include making precise generalizations to larger populations, then you may also want to use a survey to follow up on what you learn in focus groups.

The real question, however, is whether your project needs to make those kinds of generalizations. Rather than generalizing to larger populations, you may need an in-depth understanding of a particular setting or circumstance. This is where focus groups and other qualitative methods excel. For example, when the research topic involves understanding the success or failure of a particular program in a specific setting, focus groups may well be the most efficient and effective tool for uncovering the reasons behind this outcome.

Put simply, different methods have different strengths. For many purposes, the strengths of focus groups will be entirely sufficient.

Focus Groups Tell You How People Will Behave

Focus groups, individual interviews, and surveys all rely on verbal reports. They tell you how people *say* they will behave. These data thus consist of attitudes. As social psychologists know all too well, predicting behavior from attitudes is a tricky business. Often, no matter how sincerely people believe they will do something, when it comes right down to it, they do something else.

Survey researchers have had to deal with this myth for years—carefully explaining that the kinds of attitudes that surveys capture may not be strong predictors of actual behavior. The same problem occurs with focus groups. In fact, this myth may be even stronger for focus groups, since you can actually witness people saying what they will do. Not only do you get to hear people talk about their likely behavior, you can watch the group validate these statements as everyone nods and murmurs agreement. This is indeed *evidence* about how people will behave, and it can be quite compelling evidence, but it is far from conclusive.

The naive acceptance of what people say in focus groups can be quite costly. For example, in a needs assessment project, people may swear up and down that a program is essential, and then, after you go to all the trouble and expense to provide that program, they fail to use it. Any decision that is costly should be justified by more than attitudes, whether those attitudes come from focus groups or surveys. Careful pilot testing may be the only way to determine whether people's behavior will indeed correspond to their attitudes.

Some Beliefs That Should Be Encouraged

If the myths about focus groups need to be questioned, it is just as important to highlight useful ways of thinking about focus groups. Here are a few.

Be Skeptical of All Research Methods. No research method is ever perfect or foolproof, including focus groups. The purpose of this series is to explain about focus groups, not to "sell" them. Be suspicious of any expert who seems to be pushing a particular method, and be especially dubious about claims that one approach is superior to all others. Whatever method you are using, seek out researchers who balance their praise of that method's strengths with an equivalent candor about its limitations.

High-Quality Moderating Is Crucial to Focus Groups. The moderator has a major impact on the data that focus groups produce. As a result, the quality of the results are directly related to the talents, preparation, and attentiveness of this person. Just as a poorly prepared survey questionnaire can yield poor data, so to will a poorly prepared moderator. Still, moderators are not magicians, and good moderating cannot overcome the limitations of inadequate recruiting or substandard analysis. So, think of high-quality moderating as one essential ingredient in a successful focus group project.

Teamwork Produces the Best Focus Groups. Moderators often appear to be the stars of focus groups. Yet, it is equally important to have quality recruiters, note-takers, analysts, and reporters. Successful focus groups are truly a team effort, and any weak link in the chain can ruin the entire project. Getting the best results requires a concerted effort from everyone.

The Research Team Can Always Learn From the Participants. Research is all about learning from others. For a short period of time, the participants are opening their lives and sharing their experiences, preferences, and beliefs. You are there to learn from them, not to teach them something. The most destructive attitude is if the researcher thinks he or she knows more than the participants. Displays of arrogance, condescension, and superiority on the part of the researcher are sure ways to ruin a focus group. In contrast, there is nothing more delightful for a moderator than simply leaning back in your chair and listening to the participants tell you everything you ever wanted to know without your having to do a thing!

There Are Many Possible Ways to Do Focus Groups. Depending on what your purposes are, focus groups give you many options. The moderator may be either an outside professional charging thousands of dollars a day or a trained volunteer from the community. The interview may be held in a school library or a professional facility that rents for $600 a day. The participants may never have met or may all work together.

Perhaps the greatest myth is that there is "one right way" to do focus groups. We thus encourage you to find the way that is right for you—and that most definitely includes experimenting with new ways to do focus groups, rather than being bound by the existing myths.

7

What Do You Get From Focus Groups?

Overview

Reasonable Expectations
Appropriate Uses for Focus Groups
Inappropriate Uses for Focus Groups

Before you conduct focus groups, you need to consider what you will get for your efforts. This chapter begins by helping you develop reasonable expectations about what a focus group project will produce. It also gives advice on appropriate and inappropriate uses for focus groups. Overall, it provides important guidance on whether or not focus groups are right for your project.

Reasonable Expectations

Conversations are the literal data that you get from focus groups. The nature of these conversations can differ greatly from one project to the next, however. Sometimes, you want to conduct orderly interviews that follow a carefully defined agenda. Other times, your goal is to create free-flowing discussions that follow the participants' interests. Some discussions are unemotional considerations of straightforward topics. Others involve major life issues that reveal anger or pain.

It is up to you to decide what kind of conversation you want—simply planning to have a discussion is seldom enough. Instead, you need to decide what kind of discussion will work best, given both your information-gathering goals and the comfort of your participants. Ask yourself:

- How will these participants feel about this topic?
- What kinds of questions will produce the kind of discussion you desire?
- What should the moderator do or not do to manage the group dynamics?

Tape recordings and transcriptions are the most common way of converting the conversations in focus groups into analyzable data. A typical focus group lasts for 90 minutes, which amounts to over 25 pages of single-spaced transcript. Still, by themselves, the tapes or transcripts from focus groups are of little use. The real product of most focus groups is a final report, and it can take a considerable amount of analysis to convert the original conversations into a usable report. This analysis inevitably starts during the groups themselves, since what the members of the research team hear during those groups will influence the conclusions that they reach. While listening to the groups as they happen can be quite exciting, you also need to guard against getting carried away by compelling stories or rare but memorable events. You will thus need to carry out a careful and systematic analysis. During analysis, ask yourself:

- Was this topic something that came up in most of the groups?
- When it did come up, were some participants more interested in it than others?
- For people who were interested, just how important was this topic?

Analyzing and Reporting Focus Group Results Has More Information on Reporting

Although analysis can seem like a mysterious process, the key task is to shape the raw data into a report. A collection of transcripts is *not* a report, merely the starting point for one. The task of the analyst is to sort through the raw data, find the needles in the haystack, and present the needles—but not the haystack—back to the sponsor.

The style, format, and length of reports can vary considerably. One major difference in reporting style is oral versus written reports. When time is of the essence or when the sponsor's representatives can routinely attend the groups, the report may consist of oral debriefings with the moderator following each group. Some projects culminate in a major presentation by the research team; this is essentially an oral report that may be supplemented by an executive summary or other written handouts.

Analysts seldom make written reports on individual focus groups as they occur. More commonly, a final written report will crystallize the major themes that occurred across the full set of groups. When there is a well-defined interview guide for the groups, that questioning route often serves as the basic outline for organizing the report. This format allows the analyst to summarize what was learned on a question-by-question basis.

Start thinking about the ultimate report that your project will produce during the initial planning period. Ask yourself:

- Will this project produce a written or an oral report?
- Who will need to approve this report?
- What format for a report will best serve the needs of the research's sponsors?

KEY POINT

Decide on the Report Format at the Beginning of the Project

Appropriate Uses for Focus Groups

This section considers some of the situations where focus groups are a particularly desirable research method. At some level, the decision to use focus groups in a research project is a decision not to use a good many other possible research methods. In making such a decision, it is helpful to know what the advantages of focus groups are.

Consider Focus Groups When There Is a Gap Between People

A gap can occur in several ways. It might be between professionals and their target audience, between those who make decisions and those who must implement them, or between those who provide services or products and their customers. Those who manage large organizations often find that they have little understanding of the people they are trying to serve. Similarly, professionals, such as physicians, professors, teachers, architects, top-level executives, attorneys, and others, have all developed ways of thinking that may be substantially different from those of the people they need to work with.

Because the interactions in focus groups provide a window into how others think and talk, they are a powerful means of exposing the project's sponsors to the reality of those they need to understand. Sponsors often choose focus groups because this method provides immediate and vivid feedback about how others respond to their ideas. The advantages that focus groups provide for bridging such gaps help explain their popularity in such diverse applications as showing manufacturers how consumers respond to their products, helping survey researchers find appropriate questionnaire items, and providing public health workers with new insights into promoting healthy behavior.

Consider Focus Groups When Investigating Complex Behavior and Motivations

The interaction among the participants in focus groups often consists of their efforts to understand each other. The participants are curious to know how other people handle the same situations that they confront. They want to know why people like themselves do the things they do. The conversations in focus groups can thus be a gold mine of information about the ways that people behave and the motivations that underlie these behaviors. Of course, the goal of understanding complex behavior may require more than one way of finding out about that behavior, and focus groups can be combined with other methods for this purpose.

The more complex an issue is, the more difficult it is to know what questions to ask about it. Fortunately, the group discussions in focus groups allow you to hear the questions that the participants want to ask each other. This provides an excellent opportunity to uncover things that you never knew existed. At the same time, you do not surrender your own ability to ask questions. In other words, focus groups allow you both to direct the conversation toward topics that you want to investigate and to follow new ideas as they arise.

This dual ability both to direct and to follow can be especially useful for topics where people are not in touch with or able to articulate their motivations, feelings, and opinions. Many of the behaviors that researchers wish to understand are not matters of conscious importance in everyday life. As the participants in a focus group hear others talk, however, they can easily tell whether what they are hearing fits their own situation. By comparing and contrasting, they can become more explicit about their own views. In addition, they may find that answering questions from the moderator and other participants makes them aware of things that they had not thought about before.

You should not assume, however, that focus groups will always reveal deep motivational insights. They can also show that people may be less logical, less thoughtful, and less organized than you expected. By sharing their experiences with others, participants often feel free to admit things like, "I really didn't think about it. I just did it." In these circumstances, listening to focus groups can be a good antidote to the overly rational view that researchers and other professionals sometimes impose on their fellow human beings.

Consider Focus Groups When You Want to Understand Diversity

Some topics or issues are experienced differently by different people, and focus groups can help you understand the variety of others' experiences. The classic strategy for encountering diversity through focus groups creates groups that maximize the similarity of the participants within groups while emphasizing differences between groups. The fact that each group is homogeneous increases the participants' comfort in talking with similar others. The fact that the separate groups consist of different types of participants allows you to assess how similar or different the various categories of participants are.

Focus groups are thus especially useful for determining whether one set of programs will really fit all needs. Many public service agencies must fulfill the same broad mission for diverse cultural and linguistic groups. Are the things that work for one category of clients quite literally foreign to other categories of clients? Focus groups with different types of clients are an obvious way to investigate this issue. This use of focus groups also points to the possibility of understanding dimensions of diversity that go beyond ethnicity and language. Whenever you want to understand the experiences and preferences of different categories of people, comparing what they have to say in focus groups can provide valuable insights.

Consider Focus Groups When You Need a Friendly, Respectful Research Method

Focus groups have a unique ability to provide needed information as tensions between opposing parties begin to rise. When tensions are present, surveys and other means of obtaining information may be ineffective because neither party trusts the other's intentions. In contrast, focus groups convey a willingness to listen without being defensive that is uniquely beneficial in emotionally charged environments. Of course, when communication is no longer possible, it is unlikely that focus groups or any other method will work adequately.

Even in situations that are not fraught with conflict, the friendliness and respect of focus groups can be a major advantage. For the participants, this friendliness includes both an enjoyable set of interactions and a sense of being listened to. For the project's sponsors, this respect includes listening to other people's points of view in their own voices. A successful focus group project can thus forge a connection between those who commission the project and those who serve as the subjects of their investigations. Whether this helps to reduce tensions in troubled settings or simply makes people feel good about their experiences in the research process, this sense of connection can be a valuable end in itself.

Inappropriate Uses for Focus Groups

The great advantage of expanding your methodological tool kit is that new techniques allow you to do a better job of matching your tools to your needs. Still, a wise observer of research methods once remarked that a small child with a new hammer discovers that a great many things need pounding. There are already a great many things that you *can* accomplish with focus groups, but there is no point in using them to "pound on" inappropriate problems.

Avoid Focus Groups When They Imply Commitments You Cannot Keep

It is one thing when both you and the participants understand that a focus group is nothing more than a couple of hours when they talk about things that you want to know. It is quite another matter when you and the participants share a strong interest in the issues they are discussing. Asking them to tell you about their problems may imply that you are going to do something about those problems.

In essence, this is a side effect of the "friendliness" of focus groups. Friendships contain a degree of mutual obligation and commitment. Yet, all too often, the research team's commitment to a project ends with a report that includes "the voices of the community." From the community members' point of view, however, being heard may be only the first step toward actually doing something.

It is easy to say, "Don't make promises that you can't keep," but this may not be enough. Imagine the first time that you contact a group of people about participating in a focus group, and they tell you, no, they won't come because too many people have listened to them and then done nothing. Whenever you want to learn about someone's needs or problems, consider this: What are you really asking of them, and what are they expecting of you? This problem is hardly limited to focus groups, but because focus groups involve human contacts—both among the participants and between the participants and the researchers—those who use this method have a special obligation to be sensitive to the communities they work with.

Avoid Focus Groups If the Participants Are Not Comfortable With Each Other

The basic goal in conducting focus groups is to hear the participants' discussions. Groups that limit the participants' opportunity to present their own feelings, opinions, and experiences are counter to this goal. This means that focus groups are not a viable option unless the participants feel comfortable in voicing their views.

As explained in the section on group composition in *Planning Focus Groups,* it is essential that the participants in a group be compatible. This compatibility is more than a matter of demographic similarity. Each participant needs to feel that the other people around the table will understand and respect what she or he has to say.

When the participants sense that they are all similar, this will increase their comfort. When there are obvious differences among the participants, they will feel less safe in expressing themselves. For example, groups that cross authority lines are certain to make the lower-ranking participants feel uncomfortable. Hard as it may be to believe, supervisors often insist they can moderate groups made up of their employees. In reality, just knowing that their supervisor will get a report of the discussion may be enough to kill off the participants' willingness to speak freely.

Other kinds of mixed groups can be just as limiting. Occasionally, the people who commission a project will have the idea that they want to bring together opposing views. Using focus groups to create mutual understanding is laudable, as the previous section noted. Bringing hostile parties together around a table is much more problematic. This is one of those situations that might be useful for some other kind of group—such as a negotiating session—but it is not a good way to generate research data through group discussions.

Avoid Focus Groups When the Topic Is Not Appropriate for the Participants

Problems invariably arise when researchers fixate on their own interests wthout considering whether the participants will really be able to discuss the chosen topic. The match between the researchers' topics of interest and the participants' ability to discuss those topics is essential for successful focus groups. To

Planning Focus Groups Discusses Group Composition

KEY POINT

Ask: Can the Participants Really Discuss This Topic?

assess this match during the planning stages, ask the basic question, "How easy will it be to generate a free-flowing and productive conversation on this topic?"

One of the most common reasons why a topic is not appropriate is that the participants have too little involvement in it. The classic example is in comparisons of users and nonusers for some service. In the abstract, it makes perfect sense to investigate why some people use the service and others do not. Unfortunately, it is like pulling teeth to get people to talk about their lack of experience with something. Another common variation on this problem occurs when the participants have some involvement with the topic but not at the level the researchers are seeking. If your participants ever complain that you seem to be asking the same question over and over, this is a sure sign that you are too involved in the fine distinctions surrounding your topic.

It Is Difficult to Generate Conversations in Groups of "Nonusers"

Avoid Focus Groups When a Project Requires Statistical Data

Other sections in this volume have already warned against using focus groups to create statistical results, but this concern bears repeating. Undoubtedly, the most dangerous statistical misuse of focus groups comes from attempts to generalize their results to larger populations. The samples in focus groups are almost always too small and too unrepresentative to generate meaningful numbers. Focus groups emphasize depth and insight; hence, they do not employ the rigorous sampling procedures that are necessary to produce useful numerical results.

These attempts to generalize the results from focus groups confuse them with survey research, which can be generalizable when done properly. It is easy to offer the cynical speculation that attempts to cut costs are the origin of the desire to generalize from focus groups. For example, consider a political campaign that already has a compelling set of focus group results; a large-scale, well-done survey is almost certain to be expensive, so why spend the extra money? For someone with training in research methods, this question answers itself: If you believe that the conversations of 40 or 50 handpicked people can accurately represent the views of an entire electorate, then you deserve the results you get. Focus groups may be brilliant sources of insight and understanding, but they are not a substitute for solid statistical data.

Another attempt to inject statistical data into focus groups comes from project sponsors who request that a written report should give the percentage of the participants who agreed with each key conclusion. Some moderators give in to these requests by polling participants at various points during the discussion or otherwise seeking "votes" on various subjects. Voting can be a useful technique either for sparking further discussion or for determining how much consensus is present in a group, but such "data" are of little value for characterizing the beliefs of any larger population.

While reports of head counts and percentages may not be appropriate in focus group reports, limited numerical comparisons can still be useful for conveying how widespread a given experience or opinion was. Focus group reports often contain statements such as, "In every group but one, there was an extensive discussion of . . . ," or "In each group, there were at least one or two participants who . . ." These are essentially descriptive statements about what was said in the group.

These quasi-numerical descriptions should be the result of a careful "content analysis" of the group discussions, and as such, they can be an important part of the systematic examination of the data. Still, it is crucial not to confuse how often something is said with how important it is. The most important aspect of a topic may not generate more than one statement and a lot of nodding, simply because everyone in the group already knows that it is so important. Alternatively, the participants may talk a great deal about something merely because they find it interesting, not because they think it is important. Finally, if your goal is to generate ideas, the most useful idea may be said only once by one person in one group; even so, it may be exactly what you need.

*   *   *

In trying to distinguish between appropriate and inappropriate uses for focus groups, it helps to keep a basic set of principles in mind. Focus groups work best when a limited number of compatible people have the opportunity to discuss their shared interests within an open and nonthreatening environment, while guided by a skillful moderator who uses well-crafted questions. Most of these principles are flexible, but if you stray too far from the underlying purposes that they represent, you will find yourself in trouble.

Above all, remember why you are using focus groups. You are not trying to convince, teach, organize, or scold people. Instead, you are creating an excellent opportunity for others to speak and for you to listen to them.

8

Resources Required to Do Focus Groups

Overview

Planning
Recruiting
Moderating
Analyzing and Reporting
Other Costs

Conducting focus group research demands resources—specifically, time, talent, and money. These three resources are interrelated. If you don't have money, you will need to have talent. Talent can be acquired, but it takes time or money. If you have neither time, talent, nor money, you're sunk!

The resources needed for focus group research can vary considerably, depending on factors such as the location of the groups, the type of participants, the selection process for participants, and the number of groups. When estimating needed resources, it is helpful to calculate separately the needs in each of five aspects of focus group: planning, recruiting, moderating, analysis and reporting, and other costs.

Planning Focus Groups Has a Detailed Discussion of Budgets and Timelines

Planning

This category is often the most difficult to estimate. In large part, this results from the complexity of the things that need to be accomplished during the planning stage, including conceptualizing the study, developing the questions, and determining the logistical arrangements. This complexity creates difficulty in estimating the time, talent, and money associated with planning.

Issues related to time are a major source of complexity during the planning process because of the wide variation in the amount of planning time needed between one study and another. Imagine one project where an experienced focus group researcher will be doing everything—making the initial decisions, supervising the recruitment, moderating the groups, analyzing the data, and writing the report. Now imagine a project that is run by a committee. This committee will want to make and approve all the planning decisions. They will hire separate teams of people to do the recruiting, the moderating, and the analysis and report writing. Anyone who has ever done a research project that involved this kind of committee work knows full well that the initial planning process can be agonizingly slow.

Committee decision making isn't the only thing that slows down the planning process for focus groups. Some projects are just much more complex than others. Sometimes, you are working on familiar topics or interviewing groups of people that you know well, so the planning consists of variations on things you've done before. Other times, you are dealing with issues that you've never encountered before, and every problem requires a new solution.

Talent also makes a big difference in the planning process. The amount of experience and training that the members of the research team have is an obvious consideration. Less obvious is the experience level of the project sponsor. If this is the first time that someone is doing focus groups, the project may require a lot of education.

Experience can greatly affect planning, especially in writing the questions and selecting the participants. Novice focus group researchers may produce long lists of questions that cover far more topics than the group discussion can handle, or they may have questions that make perfect sense to them but are going to require a great deal of translation before the participants will be interested in them. Inexperienced researchers and sponsors may have given too little thought to whom the participants will be or how they will locate them, or they may be interested in hearing from so many different kinds of people that the costs would far exceed the budget. These issues must be dealt with during the planning process, or the price you pay later will be far higher.

Most of the money issues in the planning phase follow directly from concerns about time and talent. The longer this phase of the project is going to take or the less experience the research team has, the more it is going to cost. This is clearly one area where spending money to buy talent can be a wise investment and a real time-saver.

Planning is the fundamental first step in any project, similar to having an architect design your home. If it isn't done well, everything that follows is of questionable value. Among the resources that are necessary for good planning, talent is perhaps the most important, simply because this step is often the least structured aspect of focus groups. With talent, the process operates smoothly: The research team foresees crucial issues at the beginning of the study. They write questions that fit the study and select participants who can address these topics. The plan stays within budget. Overall, the study proceeds with harmony.

Recruiting

Recruiting participants to the focus group can occur in several ways. The recruiting can be conducted by the researcher, volunteers, or an outside group or agency. The primary means of contact will usually be by telephone or one-to-one visits. Whatever recruiting strategy you use, it requires careful attention, since poor recruitment is the Achilles' heel of focus groups. You cannot conduct a focus group without enough people, and you need to have the right people if you expect to produce a decent discussion. Even a talented moderator can do little with a handful of participants who have inadequate knowledge about the topic.

The time you spend on recruiting depends greatly on who you are trying to recruit. The efficiency of recruiting is increased when a sufficiently large pool of contacts is paired with either reasonable screening criteria for eligibility or a pre-screened list of potential participants. It also helps to have a means for direct contact, such as telephone numbers or locations where individual contact can be made. Individuals' willingness to participate is crucial. Consider whether your potential participants are "willing" prospects, who readily agree to attend the session; "hesitant" prospects, who are less willing to attend; or "difficult" prospects, who are the least willing to attend the focus group.

The talent required during recruiting includes both designing the recruitment strategy and implementing it. Designing the

Planning Focus Groups and *Involving Community Members in Focus Groups* Have More Information on Recruiting

recruitment strategy involves developing a protocol for contacting potential participants, along with screening questionnaires to find participants who meet your criteria. Implementing this strategy means using talented recruiters who make the first contact with potential participants, as well as follow-up contacts to ensure that people will attend. It thus takes one kind of skill to design a successful recruitment strategy and a different set of social skills to implement this strategy through actual contacts with participants.

Money matters in recruitment. It helps you hire teams of skilled recruiters who locate and convince the participants you need. It allows you to offer cash incentives, which is one way to overcome a low level of interest in participating. You may be fortunate enough to have an existing staff who can make the recruitment calls, along with a pool of potential participants who are highly interested in talking about your topics. If so, recruitment need not be costly. In other cases, however, spending money may be the only way to ensure that you get enough of the right people to show up for your focus groups.

Moderating

Of all the resources needed for focus groups, the easiest to estimate are those related to moderating. The time is fixed, the skills are well defined, and the pay scales are predictable. A typical focus group requires at least 3 hours of time from both the moderator and the assistant moderator. Typically, the moderating team will need to arrive at least 30 to 45 minutes before the participants arrive to set up the equipment and arrange the room. After the focus group, the moderator and assistant moderator may need to spend another 30 minutes or more in debriefing.

Chapter 6 and *Moderating Focus Groups* Have More Information on Moderating Skills

The moderating task involves certain talents and personal attributes that vary somewhat from group to group. Chapter 6 discussed both the myth that focus groups require professional moderators and the alternative myth that anyone can moderate a focus group. Depending on the project, the moderator may need to possess either training in group dynamics or background knowledge about the subject matter and participants; some projects require both kinds of skill.

The cash costs of moderating may be as low as zero, if you have talented members of your own staff. At the other end of the scale, an experienced professional moderator who is in demand within a specialized area (such as banking or high-tech engineering) may charge $2,000 a group, or more.

There are several ways that public and nonprofit organizations can save money on moderating costs. The most obvious one is to have members of their own staff trained in moderating. This amounts to paying a one-time cost to work with a professional trainer, rather than paying repeated costs to hire outside moderators. One potential compromise is to find a professional moderator who will train one or two members of your staff in the course of doing a project. Another way to reduce costs is to identify a staff member or volunteer to serve as assistant moderator. Still another option is do the analysis and report writing in-house, so that you are hiring moderators for only their most specific skills.

Be careful in making these money-saving decisions, however. For instance, if you go with the option of doing your own analysis without having the necessary talent, you are essentially wasting the entire project budget. Too often, organizations that are new to focus groups put all of their budget into hiring a professional moderator and then try to make up the difference by skimping on planning, recruitment, and analysis. This can be a recipe for disaster.

Analyzing and Reporting

Next to planning, analysis and reporting are another "black hole" for estimating time and resources. Because focus groups are an open-ended, qualitative method, you cannot predict how much effort the analysis will take. Estimates are difficult because the researcher does not know how soon or in what manner the key findings will emerge. In some studies, the analyst needs to review the tapes or transcripts multiple times, comparing different groups and the comments of different participants within groups, until the central themes emerge. In other studies, the themes and patterns emerge quickly and clearly.

Analyzing and Reporting Focus Group Results Describes Different Analysis Strategies

The resources that are required for analysis depend upon the kind of report that you want. The time, talent, and money associated with analysis all depend on the amount of depth and detail that you need in the final product. As the volume *Analyzing and Reporting Focus Group Results* describes, there several analysis strategies that rely on different kinds of data—transcripts, tapes, notes, or memory.

**Analysis
Strategies**

Transcript-Based Analysis

In this analysis option, transcripts are the primary data source. Additional data sources include field notes, debriefing discussions, oral summary statements, and other materials. This analysis strategy produces the most depth and detail; it is also the most time-consuming. The time needed to complete the analysis will vary depending on the topic, but a veteran analyst might plan to spend 8 to 12 hours per focus group in conducting the analysis and preparing the report.

Tape-Based Analysis

With tape-based analysis, the audiotapes of the focus groups are the primary data source, along with the additional data sources described above. After each group, the researcher listens to the tape and reviews the other data, often preparing an abridged transcript of the most relevant discussion. Typically, the analyst prepares a brief summary, possibly in a bulleted format, for each focus group. These individual group summaries then serve as the basis for the composite report that presents the results for the full set of focus groups. This approach requires between 4 and 8 hours per focus group.

Note-Based Analysis

With note-based analysis, the primary data source is the field notes taken during the session, typically by the assistant moderator. Often, the moderator and the assistant moderator debrief following the group, leading to either an expanded version of these notes or an additional tape recording of their debriefing discussion. Once again, the analyst prepares a summary of each focus group and then develops a composite analysis report for the full set of groups. This type of analysis may require approximately 2 to 3 hours per focus group.

Memory-Based Analysis

With memory-based analysis, the primary data source is the moderator's memory of the discussion, sometimes augmented by field notes prepared during the focus group. Such an analysis is almost always presented in oral form immediately following each group. The advantages of memory-based analysis are the immediacy and speed with which it can be provided. These oral presentations are similar to a debriefing session between the moderator and assistant moderator following the focus group, only they also involve the project sponsor. There is thus a trade-off between the reduced time and money spent on analysis versus the requirement that someone from the sponsoring organization observe each focus group and participate in the debriefing. These oral presentations usually last less than 1 hour for each focus group.

There is one other important factor that affects analysis: If the sponsor asks for recommendations, be sure to allocate additional time. Recommendations are not automatically included in a focus group report. Some sponsors are interested merely in a summary of findings, while others truly want advice on the next steps. The recommendations section of the report is that area where the research team, along with the planning committee, task force, or others who understand the organization's goals, gather to determine possible next steps for the organization. Recommendations are based on evidence presented in the focus groups, but they also take into account other factors that may influence the solution strategies, such as organizational history, resources, policy and procedures, morale, and so on.

What is a recommendation? Sometimes, there is confusion about what constitutes a recommendation. Recommendations are statements about future actions, decisions, or policies that the research team develops, based on findings from the focus group study. They are different from the recommendations that participants make during the discussion (including suggestions or advice such as, "I think they should . . .", or "It would be better if . . ."). The participants' direct statements are part of the "findings" from the study. The research team considers these statements, plus all the other data, in developing the actual recommendations.

Recommendations Take Time

Recommendations are where the results of the study are applied to real life in terms of policies and procedures. Because effective recommendations require a knowledge of the organization itself, the focus group researcher nearly always needs help from others who have this background. The extra work necessary to develop recommendations means that researchers frequently add more time to their estimates for projects that request recommendations. This extra time is needed to work with the relevant parties in reviewing the findings and crafting future directions. This process is inherently time-consuming and must be taken seriously if the report is to be useful. Recommendations that are meaningful evolve out of careful review of the data and intensive discussions.

Other Costs

Other items must be added into the cost of focus group research. Often, these factors include actual dollars, although, in the public sector, a number of these items could be donated, discounted, or borrowed from other sources. The second volume in this series, *Planning Focus Groups,* has additional information on nearly all of these items. These additional costs include the following:

***Planning Focus Groups* Has More Information on Other Costs**

- Travel expenses are incurred for the moderator team to travel to and from the focus group location. For longer distances, you may also need to pay professional consultants for the days that they spend traveling.

- Travel expenses for participants can be paid in various ways. Sometimes, travel expenses are actual costs for cabs or mileage fees. In other cases, you may simply pay participants a larger incentive fee to compensate for their travel and parking expenses.
- Recruitment charges arise when you pay someone else to recruit the participants. Many market research firms offer this service, and costs will vary depending on whether the participants you need match the people they have in their databases. These firms may charge $50 to $100 per person for relatively simple eligibility requirements in populations that are easy to locate.
- Incentives are payments or nonmonetary inducements for participating. They are also known as honorariums, stipends, or co-op fees. The amount and nature of the incentive will vary from study to study, depending on the difficulty of locating participants and inducing them to attend. The incentive should not vary within a study, however, since it is awkward and embarrassing to give differing rewards to individuals within the same focus group.
- Child care costs are necessary when conducting focus groups with parents of young children. As with travel costs, these could be included in an incentive payment that parents can use for their baby-sitting expenses. Alternatively, you can hire someone to provide child care at the focus group site. In either case, parents should be told about these opportunities in advance.
- Food costs can vary greatly, from homemade cookies that are donated to full meals at fancy restaurants.
- Room charges for a single focus group can vary from nothing to hundreds of dollars, depending on whether you need a special focus group room or are able to conduct the group in a lower-cost or free location.
- Transcription costs can vary substantially, based on the local market supply of transcribers, the length of the group, and the expertise of the transcriber. Expect to pay for 4 to 6 hours of transcribing time per hour of group discussion.
- Equipment rental or purchase can include transcription machines, computers, tape recorders, microphones, video cameras, flip charts, and so forth.
- Telephone costs occur whenever you cannot use your office phones or when you incur long-distance charges. Recruiting out-of-town participants can be especially costly.

- Office supplies, duplication, postage, tapes, batteries, and handouts are smaller budget items, but they can add up over many focus groups. Just the cost of making multiple copies of preliminary and final reports, plus postage or overnight mailing costs to sponsors or transcribers, can quickly amount to several hundred dollars.

Once you have estimated these individual items, you should also consider the need for overhead costs and contingency fees. These costs are not automatically included in the budget— indeed, some researchers always include them, and others never do. If either of these amounts is not specifically listed in the budget, then that cost is likely to be included in other line items.

- Overhead costs may include fringe benefits for employees, unbilled staff and secretarial time, and the use of office space and equipment. Depending on where you work, there may be a policy within your organization to include overhead costs in all proposals.
- Contingency fees serve as a protection from unexpected circumstances. These might include rescheduling a focus group due to "no shows," paying higher than expected recruiting fees in order to attract enough participants, and any extra costs incurred in the field. Some researchers like to build these costs into the budget as a percentage of the total cost, typically 5%.

*   *   *

The time, talent, and money required for focus group projects can and do vary considerably. Each project presents its own set of unique requirements and constraints. The time involved may be less than 2 weeks or more than 2 months. The research team may consist of in-house staff, community volunteers, or paid professionals. Similarly, the expenses can range from nothing (where all time and expenses are included in other budgets or where they are donated) to $5,000 or more for each focus group.

Ultimately, experience will be your best guide with regard to what any given project requires. If you do not have that experience yourself, then check with your colleagues who do. Just because there is no "cookie cutter" approach to estimating the resources that are necessary for focus groups doesn't mean that this has to be a guessing game.

9

It's All About Relationships
Working Together

Any focus group project will bring together sponsors, who put the project in motion; researchers, who collect and analyze the data; and participants, who provide the actual group discussions. Conducting focus groups requires paying attention not only to the needs of each of these separate parties but also to the relationships among them.

The first section of this chapter considers the basic set of relationships that connect sponsors to both researchers and participants. The subsequent sections on researchers and participants cover special concerns about the relationships that affect each of these roles.

Sponsors

The sponsors are the ones who commission the research. The people sponsoring the project both set the initial goals and receive the final report. The sponsors may or may not be active in the day-to-day life of the project, but their roles at the beginning and end of the project are unmistakable.

In the marketing literature, sponsors are often referred to as "clients." This reflects the fact that most of this literature is written from the point of view of private consultants, who consider the people they are working for to be their clients. In the public sector, however, clients are typically the people who re- ceive the services that these organizations offer. To avoid confusion, the books in this kit refer to the people in charge of the overall project as the sponsors—a usage that also better captures the role that these people play in the project.

Relationships Between Sponsors and Researchers

There are several different configurations for the relationship between sponsors and researchers. This section will concentrate on projects where sponsors hire outside researchers. In this case, there is a clear separation between the sponsors, who define the objectives for the project, and the researchers, who collect and analyze the data. In other types of projects, the sponsors and the researchers are the same people. In that case, the people defining the goals of the project also have responsibility for carrying them out. Still another type of project relies on community volunteers, so there is often a professional researcher who provides guidance to the team, even though the community members themselves typically determine the purposes of the project and have the primary responsibility for carrying it out. This configuration, in which the researcher assists community members who are both sponsors and researchers, receives special treatment in the final volume of this kit.

The prototypical relationship between sponsors and outside researchers is a contractual one, where the sponsors hire the researchers. The decision to hire outside researchers may be motivated by several factors, including the lack of internal staff to conduct the study, the need to produce high-quality data, or the desire to have a neutral party conduct the study. In focus groups, these outside researchers are commonly referred to as "moderators," although they may also develop the recruitment strategy, write the questions in the interview guide, analyze the data, and generate the final report.

Involving Community Members in Focus Groups Describes a Different Relationship Between Sponsors and Researchers

For better or worse, sponsors have considerable leeway in how they oversee the researchers' performance of these activities. In some cases, sponsors are too quick to turn everything over to a "professional." Although this can save planning time at the beginning of the project, it often produces other headaches later on. At its worst, this kind of relationship leaves the sponsors with expensive but irrelevant data. In other cases, sponsors insist on micro-managing decisions that they don't understand. Despite all the time and effort that goes into this ill-informed guidance, the actual products typically look little different from what the researcher would have done with far fewer meetings, faxes, and phone calls. At its worst, this kind of relationship leads researchers to give in to the sponsor's dubious suggestions, since there is no point in "trying to save them from themselves."

A group of academic researchers received a large grant to implement a nationwide program. They decided to use "before and after" surveys as the primary means for determining how well the program worked, and they decided to use focus groups to help write the surveys. Because they had never used focus groups, they hired a well-known marketing research firm to do this part of the work.

During the focus groups, there was very little communication between the university-based researchers who were sponsoring the project and the marketing researchers who were conducting the groups. Still, the sponsors were initially pleased when the researchers gave them a thick report, plus transcripts and videotapes, from more than 20 focus groups conducted nationwide. Unfortunately, they quickly realized that the hired researchers had never properly understood the nature of the program that the sponsors were designing. In fact, despite its length, the final report contained very little of the information that the sponsors had been expecting to receive. Their only hope was to hire a new consultant to help them reanalyze the data, in the belief that what they wanted was "somewhere in all those focus groups."

EXAMPLE

Too Little Communication Between Sponsors and Researchers

Just as in the rest of life, good relationships between sponsors and researchers are based on mutual understanding. Researchers should not automatically assume that they understand what the sponsors want; instead, they should seek explicit confirmation of how well they comprehend the sponsors' goals. Similarly, sponsors have a responsibility to understand what the researchers will and will not deliver. Producing mutually acceptable results begins with establishing mutual understanding.

Mutual respect is just as important. Researchers should never assume that their greater experience means that they know more about what the sponsors want than the sponsors do. Similarly,

Chapter 10 Discusses Ethical Issues Between Sponsors and Researchers

sponsors should not treat researchers as servants who are paid to do their masters' bidding. Creating a successful match between the sponsors' purposes and the researchers' results requires each side to respect what the other brings to their joint enterprise.

It is also important to note that the connection between sponsors and hired researchers is a business relationship. Often, there will be a legally binding contract that spells out many aspects of this relationship. In addition, there will be ethical issues that affect the exchanges between sponsors and researchers, as discussed in the next chapter.

The Relationship Between the Sponsor and the Participants

The connection between the sponsors and the researchers typically receives the most attention; while that relationship is vital, the relationship between the sponsors and the participants can be just as important. This is particularly true when there is an ongoing relationship between the project's sponsors and the participants. These continuing connections are most likely to occur when you are conducting focus groups within an organization, but ongoing relationships between sponsors and participants can also occur in a variety of other settings.

Learn to Recognize When Relationships Exist

Such ongoing relationships require careful thought that takes into account both the past and the future. Past relationships create a shared history that can affect every aspect of the research, including what questions you ask and how you ask them, as well as the assumptions that the participants bring to the session. Future relationships mean shared commitments that may be affected by what happens in the current focus groups.

During the planning stages of a project, when you are identifying whom the participants will be, consider whether they have ongoing relationships with the project's sponsors. Recruiting the participants from a preexisting list is a simple sign of an ongoing relationship. Whenever the sponsors can supply a list of potential participants, this signals the kind of prior contact that can also have future implications. Such lists often provide a concrete starting point for exploring the relationship between the sponsors and the participants. Useful questions to consider include the following:

Planning Focus Groups **Discusses Using Existing Lists in Recruitment**

- How did the list come into being?
- Who is on the list?
- Who is not on the list or excluded from it?

As the following chapter on ethics emphasizes, the most basic question is whether *anything* about the project could affect the relationship between the sponsor and the participants. The content of the interview questions has the biggest influence on how participants perceive the project, but many other factors can also affect the impressions that participants carry away. For example:

Chapter 10 Discusses Ethical Issues in the Relationship Between Sponsors and Participants

- Who will be selected to participate and who will not? Is there a danger that some categories of potential participants will feel excluded?
- Where will the groups be held? Will a neutral setting encourage more open discussions?
- Who will moderate the groups? Will an outsider know enough about the local situation? Will the participants believe that someone from the sponsoring organization can be objective?
- What kinds of outcomes will the participants expect from the groups? Is there a danger that just holding the groups will create unrealistic expectations for results?

Consider the case of a large organization that was planning major changes in its benefits package that would affect all employees. To gauge employee reaction, the company planned for a series of focus groups to be held on company time. To minimize the disruption in work schedules, the planners set aside 1-hour time blocks, based on a 45-minute discussion and 15 minutes to move back and forth between job sites and the conference room where the focus groups were held.

Now, put down the book, and think about the impressions that this project might have had on the employees. What potential dangers might there be in this plan?

EXERCISE

Avoiding Unintended Impressions

One basic problem with this project was that it emphasized management's information needs while giving too little attention to the company's ongoing relationship with its employees. The upper-level managers who were planning the project were sure that they could hear all they needed to hear in groups that lasted 45 minutes, but would employees feel that this short time gave them a chance to say everything they wanted to? A major change in their benefits could be quite controversial. Hence, from a relationship standpoint, longer groups might have been advisable, even if they were not necessary for information gathering and even if this extra time commitment had short-term costs.

Also, what about rumor control? If only a small percentage of the total employees participated, what might others have heard secondhand or thirdhand? A simple information sheet that each participant could take away would minimize the spread of misinformation.

One special case involves projects where the relationship between the sponsor and the participants is the topic of the research itself. Customer satisfaction is a common example of such a project. In this instance, it is especially important not to oversell the potential outcomes of the research. From the sponsor's point of view, simply talking to the participants may be a sufficient sign of interest and respect. From the participants' point of view, however, the lack of any immediate response from the sponsors may suggest that no one is really listening to them.

Research on customer satisfaction and related topics has to be especially careful not to create disappointments by raising expectations. During the planning process, thinking about ongoing relationships can highlight questions such as the following:

- Will the research project provide direct benefits for these participants?
- If outcomes will occur, when will they happen?
- If the participants are disappointed, what effects might this have?

Who Else Has a Stake?

The sponsors, the researchers, and the participants are the most obvious stakeholders in a focus group project, but who else might have an interest? Are there other groups and organizations in the community who might care about the project? This can be an important concern because participants may talk to a wide range of other people about their experiences in the focus group. If the topic of the groups is truly of interest to the participants, then you can bet they will tell others about it.

Too often, researchers and sponsors think of the participants solely in terms of their relationship to the immediate project, but most participants actually have extensive contacts throughout their communities. What might others hear, secondhand, about this project?

Part of the initial planning process should thus include asking who else might have a stake in this topic and how these relationships should be taken into account.

Researchers

In most focus group projects, the researchers are the connection between the sponsor and the participants. Ordinarily, the sponsors will have no direct contact with the participants. This means that the researchers must not only maintain relationships with both the sponsors and the participants but also broker the more indirect relationship between the other two parties. It is easy to overlook the researchers' role in creating and maintaining relationships, especially if you think of them simply as "moderators." One way to clarify the role of researchers is to realize that the actual focus groups fall midway between determining the topics and summarizing the results.

In many ways, the researchers' job is to bridge the gap between the world of the sponsors and the world of the participants. Part of this bridging function occurs in writing the questions, which must both meet the sponsors' needs and make sense to the participants. During the groups themselves, moderators need to strike a balance between hearing what participants have to say and getting them to talk about the issues that interest the sponsors. Finally, in analysis and reporting writing, researchers need to attend to both the sponsors' purposes for the project and the participants' point of view on these issues.

Researchers thus have a dual role. Indeed, this duality may be the key function that the researchers perform in a focus group project. If focus groups are all about listening and learning, it is the researchers' job to help the sponsors listen to and learn from the participants. Yet, it is the researchers who actually have the most direct contact with both the sponsors and the participants. In essence, the researchers stand at the midpoint of a communication process that must move back and forth between the projects' sponsors and the participants. A successful linkage between the researchers' relationships with both sponsors and participants is the essential glue that holds a focus group project together.

Participants

The previous sections have already covered the participants' relationships with both the sponsors and the researchers, but there is at least one more topic to be covered: the participants' relationships among themselves.

Chapter 10
Discusses Ethical
Aspects of
Relationships
Among
Participants

When the participants already have ongoing relationships, this creates a set of ethical issues that are covered in the next chapter. When the project's sponsor is a community organization or government agency, the participants may well be acquainted. Projects that involve program planning or evaluation are especially likely to bring together participants who already know each other. Privacy is an especially important concern in such groups, since any information that is revealed in the discussion may have lasting implications.

When the participants know each other, this affects the kinds of topics that the discussion will cover and how these issues will be raised. Ongoing relationships among the participants also affect the way that the moderator interacts with them. For example, if acquaintances share a set of taken-for-granted assumptions about the topic, then the project planning should emphasize questions and moderating strategies that will bring these assumptions out in the open.

Case 3 in
Chapter 3
Includes an
Example of
Mobilization

Groups where the participants are not acquainted can still raise relationship issues. In particular, you need to be attentive to circumstances where conducting focus groups can create relationships. Focus groups are especially likely to create new relationships when the participants have common interests. This unusual opportunity to discuss ideas with like-minded others can be quite energizing. Such groups may even "mobilize" participants to stay in contact and thus create ongoing relationships among the participants. Case 3 in Chapter 3 includes an example of mobilization among the participants.

The most obvious sign of mobilization is that the participants start asking for each others' names and phone numbers. If participants do seek to keep in touch with each other, it is best not to interfere with this process. Any attempt to stifle these processes, once they are in motion, is almost certain to produce resistance and resentment. From a researcher's standpoint, the best strategy is to meet with the projects' sponsors to discuss, in advance, whether mobilization is likely to happen. If mobilization is likely, the research team will need a way to inform the sponsors when it has occurred. Then, if these newly energized participants contact the sponsors, this will not come as a surprise; in fact, this prior planning may allow the sponsors to be ready with an appropriate response.

Interfering With
Attempts to
Mobilize Can
Make Things
Worse

* * *

From an instrumental point of view, focus groups are an exercise in information gathering. In practice, however, they are all about relationships. The focus group discussion itself is a set of temporary relationships, but the larger project also involves a series of more fateful relationships. Often, projects involving focus groups are designed in the hope of having long-lasting effects, and this process of making a difference may begin with the relationships in the project itself.

10

Ethical Issues

Overview

Are Participants "At Risk"?
Privacy: Basic Issues
Privacy: The Sponsor's Relationship to the Participants
Privacy: What the Participants Learn About Each Other
Dealing With Stressful Topics
Setting Boundaries
Protecting the Sponsor's Privacy

Most of the ethical issues in focus groups flow from relation-ships: What obligations do the sponsor and the researcher have to the participants? What obligations do the participants have to each other? Hence, the material in the previous chapter provides a valuable starting point for the consideration of ethical issues in focus groups.

In thinking about ethical issues, it helps to keep them in perspective. Although this is the longest chapter in this book, most projects involving focus groups actually pose few ethical issues. Still, when ethical issues do arise, they require careful attention.

Are Participants "At Risk"?

As in medicine, the first rule in focus groups is: Do no harm. If your work will be reviewed by a Human Subjects Research

Review Committee, it will define the issues you need to address. Even if your research will not be reviewed by a human subjects committee, it is still necessary to consider the ethical question that is at the heart of those reviews: Does this project put the participants at risk?

BACKGROUND

Risk in Research Involving Human Subjects

According to the federal guidelines for human subjects, risk occurs under the following conditions:

1. *The participants are unable to provide legal statements of informed consent. This applies to anyone under the age of 18, as well as many institutional populations.*
2. *Any disclosure of the human subjects' responses outside the research could reasonably subject the participants to criminal or civil liability or could damage the subjects' financial standing, employability, or reputation.*

Note that these conditions are not meant to be exhaustive. Whenever either of these conditions applies, then issues of risk *must* be reviewed in settings that have a human subjects committee. These two items are always a good starting point in considering possible risks, but there may be other sources of risk in any given project. Whether your project will be reviewed by an outside committee or not, it is up to you to think through *all* the ways that the participants might be at risk.

Whenever a review committee determines that a research project will put the participants at risk, the researcher must provide a "Statement of Informed Consent" to the participants. Such statements tell the participants about both the potential risks in the project and their rights as participants in the project.

EXAMPLE

Sample of a Statement of Informed Consent

Statement of Informed Consent

I, _____, agree to participate in this research project on "[title of project]" that is being conducted by [researcher's name] from [sponsoring organization].

I understand that the purpose of this study is to hold a group interview to find out about [research topic]; we will discuss our general ideas about [topics].

I understand that the study involves a focus group interview that lasts two hours or less, which will be audiotaped.

I understand that my participation in this study is entirely voluntary, and that if I wish to withdraw from the study or to leave, I may do so at any time, and that I do not need to give any reasons or explanations for doing so. If I do withdraw from the study, I understand that this will have no effect on my relationship with [sponsor] or any other organization or agency.

I understand that because of this study, there could be violations of my privacy. To prevent violations of my own or others' privacy, I have been asked not to talk about any of my own or others' private experiences that I would consider too personal or revealing.

I also understand that I have an obligation to respect the privacy of the other members of the group by not disclosing any personal information that they share during our discussion.

I understand that all the information I give will be kept confidential to the extent permitted by law, and that the names of all the people in the study will be kept confidential.

I understand that I may not receive any direct benefit from participating in this study, but that my participation may help others in the future.

The members of the research team have offered to answer any questions I may have about the study and what I am expected to do.

I have read and understand this information and I agree to take part in the study.

———————————   ——————————————————————————————

Today's Date   *Your Signature*

If you have concerns or questions about this study, please contact either [researcher's name and telephone number] or the chair of the Human Subjects Research Review Committee, [location and phone number].

Privacy: Basic Issues

Focus groups inevitably involve the sharing of information; hence, privacy is one of the central ethical concerns in focus group research. The crucial ethical issue in protecting the participants' privacy is, Who will have access to what the participants say during their discussions?

The first step in protecting privacy is to restrict access to information that reveals the participants' identities. Official reviews of research involving human subjects make a careful distinction between projects that offer participants true anonymity versus those that promise to protect their confidentiality. *Anonymity* means that there is no way to identify who the participants were. Few focus group projects qualify as offering true anonymity.

Instead, it is more common to promise *confidentiality*, which means that identifying information will be gathered, but it will be carefully protected.

BACKGROUND

Anonymity Versus Confidentiality

The following steps help in guaranteeing confidentiality:

- *Once recruitment is completed, only the researcher will have access to any of the recruitment information, and these records will be destroyed at the conclusion of the project.*

- *During the discussion, participants will be identified only by first names or pseudonyms.*

- *Once transcription is complete, only the researchers will have access to the tapes that were made, and these tapes will be destroyed at the conclusion of the project.*

- *For any transcripts that are made, not only names but any other potentially identifying information (e.g., mentions of specific individuals, events, or places) will be either removed or modified.*

In practice, a commitment to maintain confidentiality means that it is acceptable to collect potentially damaging information, so long as no one other than the researcher can identify specific participants. Procedures for maintaining confidentiality must ensure that participants can safely share their experiences and opinions without having their statements used against them. It is the researcher's responsibility to devise such procedures and carry them out.

EXAMPLE

Protecting Confidentiality

Kerth O'Brien (1993) conducted focus groups with gay and bisexual men to learn about their responses to the AIDS epidemic. Because these discussions involved revelations about sexual orientation and HIV status, it was imperative to protect the participants' confidentiality. As a first step in protecting the identity of the participants, the Human Subjects Review Committee approved procedures that avoided collecting traditional signed statements of informed consent. Instead, the researcher began each tape recording by reading the statement of informed consent, followed by each participant's stating his first name (or a pseudonym) and affirming that he understood the statement of consent and agreed to it. In addition, the recruiting materials, tape recordings, and other records were locked in a safe that was specially purchased for the project and stored away from the researcher's main office. Furthermore, much of the recruiting was done over a dedicated, private phone line. Although such intense efforts to maintain confidentiality are certainly rare, they are especially important whenever focus groups truly do put participants at risk.

A further threat to privacy arises from the fact that focus groups frequently include tape recordings. Who will have access to these tapes? Will they ever be played in public? The range of people who are interested in a project can be surprising, and the temptation to play tapes can be very real. The simplest rule to consider here is whether sharing this information might put participants at risk in any way. Are the participants potentially identifiable? Do the discussions involve sensitive or emotional issues? As a practical example, one trainer sometimes shows segments from videotapes during workshops for new moderators, so long as the tapes are more than 2 years old, were made in another city, and do not involve controversial topics.

Privacy: The Sponsor's Relationship to the Participants

One of the chief concerns in protecting the participants' privacy is what the sponsor will learn about the participants. Of course, the sponsor's desire for information from the participants is what drives the research, but this does not give the sponsor unlimited access to what the participants say. This is a special concern whenever there is an ongoing relationship between the sponsor and the participant, as discussed in Chapter 9. When the sponsor and the participants will have future contacts, there is a risk that participants will reveal information that might damage their ongoing relationship with the sponsor.

Chapter 9 Discusses the Sponsor's Relationship With Participants

Although it is easy, in theory, to devise procedures that will keep the identity of individual participants confidential, sponsors and other interested parties may be hungry for precisely this information. This is especially true when the focus groups generate negative information. Almost every veteran focus group researcher has had to confront an angry sponsor who has just read a report and wants to know exactly which participant made some particularly negative remark. No matter how much sponsors insist up front that they want the whole truth, warts and all, it is only human nature for them to want to confront their critics. For example, when asked about her worst experience in a focus group, one very experienced researcher related the story of a sponsor who ran out from behind a one-way mirror to lecture the participants on how mistaken they were about his company and its services!

In practical terms, working with sponsors to protect the participants' privacy means reaching an explicit agreement, before the groups occur, about any potentially identifying information that the sponsor will receive:

- Will the sponsor observe the groups?
- Will the sponsor see videotapes of the participants?
- Will the sponsor receive a list of the names of participants?
- Will the sponsor receive transcripts of the groups, even with names deleted?

EXAMPLE

Focus Groups as Industrial Espionage

What do you do when the sponsor's main intent in the project is to get information to use against the participants? This issue came up with a manufacturing firm that wanted to do focus groups among their major suppliers. The principal goal was to learn which factors affected the suppliers' pricing policies, so that the manufacturer could negotiate more favorable contracts.

It is obvious why a company would want to conduct research on this topic, but it is just as obvious why the participants would want to keep this information private. Attempting to obtain information that others wish to protect is a form of industrial espionage. Participating in a project such as this could put you at risk of civil or even criminal prosecution. A useful source for guidance with regard to this and similar issues in business ethics is Lawrence Chonko's (1995) Ethical Decision Making in Marketing.

Privacy: What the Participants Learn About Each Other

A different privacy issue concerns what the participants learn about each other. Group interviews are unique as a research method because information is shared not only with the researcher but also with the other participants. This might not present a problem if every participant simply took responsibility for maintaining her or his own privacy during the discussions. In reality, the dynamics of self-disclosure in focus groups are much trickier.

KEY POINT

Focus Groups Can Produce Over-Disclosure

Every interaction involves a degree of self-disclosure, that is, the amount that people reveal about themselves in the course of a conversation. The degree of self-disclosure that people do depends a great deal on whom they are talking with. For example, people may reveal quite different attitudes toward their work, depending on whether they are talking to their family or their boss. The setting for the conversation can also make a big difference. The things you might say in a supermarket check-out line are different from what you might share in a dimly lit restaurant. From an ethical standpoint, focus group researchers need to consider what is an appropriate level of self-disclosure. In particular, there is a very real danger of over-disclosure, that is, participants regretting that they revealed as much as they did.

In a focus group, if just one person reveals some potentially damaging personal fact or dangerously strong opinion without causing a disruption in the discussion, this creates the potential for over-disclosure. When others realize it is "safe" to discuss such ordinarily taboo topics, they may well add their own disclosures. Indeed, in the heat of the moment, such dramatic revelations may feel thrilling to the participants.

Over-disclosure is an especially serious threat to privacy when there are ongoing relationships among the participants, since this information can influence their future dealings with each other. The most effective way to deal with this problem is to call attention to it, right from the start. Your introduction to the group should remind the participants that they already know each other and that their contacts with each other will continue after this group is over. When over-disclosure among participants who know each other is a concern, one useful strategy is to ask the group to make up its own ground rules for protecting privacy. This involves setting aside about 5 minutes during the introduction for the participants to brainstorm about how they will limit what they disclose about themselves and others.

TIP

Ask Participants to Set Their Own Rules on Self-Disclosure

Interestingly, over-disclosure is most likely to be a problem in focus groups among strangers, especially when they know that they will meet for only a single session. This approximates an unusual self-disclosure setting known as "strangers on a train" (although, today, "strangers on a plane" might be more realistic). This captures the experience that talking with someone you will never see again can lead to self-disclosure that goes beyond what you would tell your friends and family. In other words, the conversation that you have with the stranger seated next to you on an airplane, or at a focus group, may be much more revealing than the one you might have with someone with whom you have an ongoing relationship. Thus, there is a special concern for over-disclosure in focus groups that (1) bring together strangers, (2) for a single session, (3) to discuss emotional or controversial topics. The best way to deal with this problem is to plan for it by setting conscious limits on how far the discussion should go. The section in this chapter on setting boundaries provides suggestions for avoiding problems of over-disclosure.

Dealing With Stressful Topics

Creating stress is one way that focus groups can put participants at risk. Many community-based focus groups involve topics that are emotionally stressful, such as alcohol and drug use, chronic illnesses, poverty, family violence, and sexual behavior. Participants often welcome the opportunity to talk about these topics with others who share their experiences, but that does not mean that these discussions are not stressful. Focus groups on emotional topics can be both very rewarding and very stressful.

A simple strategy for thinking about stress is to ask whether the focus group discussions will be any more stressful than what the participants would experience in their ordinary lives. Is this the most stressful thing that might happen to them during the next 2 or 3 days? If not, you may have little to worry about. If so, then you should think about how to lower stress levels or how to make them more manageable.

**Thinking About
Stress Levels**

When stress is an unavoidable aspect of a project, here are some tactics for managing it:

- Emphasize that participation is completely voluntary and that no one is obligated to answer any of the questions that you ask.

- Tell participants that they are free to take a break or leave at any time if they feel uncomfortable, and that they do not need to offer any explanation if they cease participating.

- Prepare an information sheet for the participants, including relevant agencies and referral sources, in case the discussion raises issues that they wish to pursue further.

- Try to include someone on the research team who has experience with these sources of stress, either in his or her personal life or as a counselor.

- If no one in the team has enough experience with these sources of stress, then meet with a support group or counselors who can sensitize you to the relevant issues.

- In extreme cases, have a trained professional either present or on call.

**Managing a
Potentially
Stressful
Discussion**

In a series of focus groups with women who had been widowed within the past 3 to 6 months (Morgan, 1989), our research team realized that this experience had dominated their daily lives. Even so, a 2-hour conversation about their bereavement would be an unusual and potentially stressful experience for most of these women.

We began by raising the issue of stress in the introduction to each group. We told the participants that our desire to hear from them was not nearly as important as their own comfort, given everything that they had been through. So, if they felt at all uncomfortable or stressed, they should take a break or even leave the group. We also told them that their first priority should be to take care of themselves and each other, and that they should not, under any circumstances, subject themselves to stress in an effort to help us.

In addition, one member of the project learned about services that were available to recent widows in the local area and prepared an informational handout for the participants. In the introduction to each group, we showed this handout to the participants and *told them they would each receive a copy at the end of the discussion. We did not want to distribute this information at the beginning of the session, since it might distract participants from our central topics. We also made sure that we gave a copy to everyone, so that no one would feel "singled out" as especially needy.*

Setting Boundaries

It is the researcher's responsibility to minimize both stressful situations and invasions of privacy. This requires you to set boundaries that define the acceptable limits of the discussion *in advance*. This planning allows you to recognize a potentially stressful situation as soon as it starts to occur. Similarly, advance planning will help prevent invasions of privacy before people say things that they can't take back.

Setting boundaries on stress requires recognizing the early signs of stress. After you ask a question that is potentially stressful, you need to invoke a conscious monitoring process throughout that portion of the discussion. Here are some signs that you are reaching the boundary on stress and that you should pull the discussion back to a safer place:

Setting Boundaries for Stress

- Has someone pulled back from the table?
- Are people either huddling together or withdrawing from each other?
- Do you hear voices "cracking" or stuttering?
- Is someone becoming red in the face or short of breath?

Setting boundaries on privacy and self-disclosure requires putting yourself in the place of the participants. A useful way to do this is to imagine how participants will feel the morning after the group: Will they regret having disclosed too much? The goal in setting a boundary on self-disclosure should be to ensure that no one wakes up the next day feeling bad about what he or she said in your focus group.

Setting Boundaries for Privacy

One of the most effective ways to deal with potential breaches of ethical boundaries is to raise this issue right from the start. Thus the moderator's introduction can include a statement such as the following:

"Some of the topics that you'll be discussing today can be very sensitive and personal. We don't want you to say anything that you might regret later. And we don't want you to feel stressed by this discussion. So, if I sense that the discussion is getting too stressful or too personal, I'll have us all take a little break, relax for a minute, and then start up again at a level where everyone feels comfortable."

Moderators Should Set Boundaries Early

Later, if stress or privacy concerns do reach a boundary, the moderator has created a basis for refocusing the discussion:

"Let's stop for a minute. Back at the start, I mentioned that we might get into areas that were too sensitive or personal. I don't think we're there yet, but I'm concerned that we might be headed that way. Why don't you all sit back in your seats, take a deep breath, and relax for a second. And then we'll come back to the general topic of . . ."

Assistant Moderators Can Help Monitor Boundaries

Monitoring ethical boundaries during discussions can be difficult, even for skilled moderators. There is so much going on in a focus group that it is easy to miss the fact that someone is showing signs of stress, or that a seemingly casual remark has opened the door for over-disclosure. Having a well-trained assistant in the room is thus especially valuable. By tradition, the assistant sits across the room from the moderator. When it is necessary to monitor ethical boundaries, it helps to have prearranged signals that the assistant can use to get the moderator's attention. A small hand motion is usually sufficient, since the assistant ordinarily does as little as possible to draw attention to himself or herself. If necessary, starting to stand up will almost certainly make the moderator aware of the need to pause and refocus the discussion.

Protecting the Sponsor's Privacy

Ethical issues in focus groups are not entirely limited to protecting participants. The relationship between the sponsor and researcher can also raise concerns, especially with respect to the privacy of the information that focus groups generate. This private information is variously referred to as *intellectual property, proprietary knowledge,* or *trade secrets.* Obviously, issues relating to the protection of such information occur most frequently when working with private companies, especially in projects that involve product marketing. Government agencies and community organizations may also need to keep information private, however, especially in projects that involve changing existing services or creating new ones.

Concerns about protecting the sponsor's privacy are especially acute for consultants, since they may later work for a competing organization. In that case, it helps if the researcher is proactive and raises these issues right from the start. Those who encounter this problem repeatedly would be wise to prepare a standard confidentiality agreement that they and the sponsor can sign. Such agreements also typically contain statements about rights with regard to new ideas, including patents and copyrights.

Although some sponsors may already have such agreements of their own, these can be highly restrictive and thus should be carefully scrutinized. If these issues are likely to be a common feature of your own work, you should definitely seek competent legal advice.

This agreement acknowledges that during the course of this work [consultant] may have access to information that [sponsor] considers to be its intellectual property, trade secret, or proprietary knowledge. As part of this agreement, [sponsor] accepts the obligation to designate, in advance, any information that [consultant] should treat as confidential. In turn, [consultant] agrees to protect the information that [sponsor] designates as private. In particular, [consultant] will not make use of or otherwise disclose such designated information without the express written permission of [sponsor], except as required by law.

This work may also result in the development of new information that [sponsor] considers to be its intellectual property, trade secret, or proprietary knowledge, including ideas and inventions that are subject to patents and/or copyrights. [Sponsor] agrees to define, in advance, any areas where such ideas and information may arise. In turn, the [consultant] agrees to inform the [sponsor] in a timely fashion about any new information that this project acquires or develops in these designated areas. In addition, [consultant] agrees to assign the rights for patents or copyrights related to these designated areas of activity, without additional charges, to [sponsor]. In turn, [sponsor] agrees to bear all expenses involved in obtaining any patents or copyrights related to these designated areas.

EXAMPLE

A Sample Agreement of Confidentiality

One special case related to protecting the sponsors' privacy occurs when they do not want their identity revealed to the participants. A basic principle in this regard is that deception is not acceptable. Withholding the sponsor's identity is one thing, but leading the participants to believe that someone else is sponsoring the research is something quite different.

Often, sponsors request that their identity be withheld without considering the impact that this can have on the discussion. If the topic is at all intriguing, participants will probably try to guess who the sponsor is. Such hidden assumptions by participants can affect what they say in ways that are hard to detect. If the participants are likely to engage in this kind of guesswork, the sponsor needs to decide whether protecting their identity is worth the cost of producing lower-quality data.

A common solution to this dilemma is the promise to reveal the project's sponsor at the end of the focus group. This approach is particularly useful when the participants will be comparing several competing versions of a service or product. In this scenario,

EXAMPLE

**Revealing a
Sponsor's Identity**

the participants first make general comparisons among all the alternatives; then, after, the sponsor's identity is revealed, they give more specific feedback on that product or service.

Imagine an example in which the sponsor is a major travel agency that wants to revamp its basic brochures and promotional materials. First, the participants compare a series of brochures from several different travel agencies, including the sponsor's existing materials. After the participants discuss their basic reactions to the materials, the moderator passes out index cards and asks each person to write down his or her best guess about which agency is the sponsor. After hearing their guesses, the moderator reveals who the sponsor is and tells the group that the sponsor is planning to revise its brochures. What advice can the group give? What are some of the best features of the sponsor's current brochures that it should keep? What are some positive aspects of the other agencies' brochures that it might incorporate? Note that asking the participants to guess who the sponsor is provides potentially useful information about the assumptions that participants were making in the earlier portion of their discussions.

* * *

Overall, ethical issues touch each of the major parties in a focus group project. Sponsors have an ethical responsibility to protect the rights of participants but also have rights of their own that need to be protected. Similarly, the participants have both rights and responsibilities. They have a right to understand any risks involved in the project, they have a right to confidentiality, and they should experience a minimum of stress. The participants' responsibilities touch on many of the same issues. In particular, participants need to be aware that stressful situations and invasions of privacy can arise from the things that they themselves do during the group discussions.

Ultimately, however, the research team has the job of upholding all these rights and responsibilities. Think of your efforts to address ethical issues as an "ounce of prevention." Given the serious problems that can arise, you will definitely want to avoid a "pound of cure."

11

Checklist
Are Focus Groups Right for You?

Use focus groups when:

- Your goal is to listen to and learn from other people (Chapter 2).

- You can explore the topics that interest you through conversations among the participants (Chapter 2).

- You can obtain in-depth knowledge by listening as the participants share and compare their experiences, feelings, and opinions (Chapter 2).

- You can pursue interpretive questions about "how and why" through group discussions (Chapter 2).

- Your purpose is to identify problems that you need to address (Chapter 2).

- Your purpose is to plan for programs, survey questionnaires, quality initiatives, and so on (Chapter 2).

- Your purpose is to improve the implementation of a project (Chapter 2).

- Your purpose is to assess the outcome of a program or intervention (Chapter 2).

- You want to understand or reduce a gap in understanding between groups of people (Chapter 7).

- You are researching complex behaviors and motivations (Chapter 7).

- You want to understand diversity (Chapter 7).

- You need a friendly, respectful research method (Chapter 7).

- You have a team of people who all want to work together so the project's sponsors can better understand the people who participate in the focus groups (Chapter 9).

Avoid focus groups when:

- Your goals are something other than research—such as selling, educating, negotiating, or decision making (Chapter 4).

- You cannot hold a focused discussion, due to either the breadth of your topic or the size of your group (Chapter 4).

- You will not carry on meaningful discussions in the groups you bring together (Chapter 4).

- Your driving motivation is to save time and money (Chapter 6).

- You need strong predictions about how people will behave (Chapter 6).

- Your asking to hear from people will imply commitments to them that you cannot keep (Chapter 7).

- You want to bring together participants who are not comfortable with each other (Chapter 7).

- Your topic is something that the participants are not really capable of talking about (Chapter 7).

- You need statistical data (Chapter 7).

- Your topic will create serious invasions of privacy (Chapter 10).

- Your topic will create unacceptable levels of stress (Chapter 10).

References

Chonko, L. (1995). *Ethical decision making in marketing*. Thousand Oaks, CA: Sage.

Folch-Lyon, E., Macorra, L., & Schearer, S. B. (1981). Focus group and survey research on family planning in Mexico. *Studies in Family Planning, 12,* 409-432.

Goldman, A. E., & McDonald, S. S. (1987). *The group depth interview: Principles and practice.* Englewood Cliffs, NJ: Prentice Hall.

Joseph, J. G., Emmons, C. A., Kessler, R. C., Wortman, C. B., O'Brien, K. J., Hocker, W. T., & Schaefer, C. (1984). Coping with the threat of AIDS: An approach to psychosocial assessment. *American Psychologist, 39,* 1297-1302.

Knodel, J. (1995). Focus groups as a method for cross-cultural research in social gerontology. *Journal of Cross-Cultural Gerontology, 10,* 7-20.

Krueger, R. A. (1994). *Focus groups: A practical guide for applied research* (2nd ed.). Thousand Oaks, CA: Sage.

Lofland, J., & Lofland, L. H. (1995). *Analyzing social settings: A guide to qualitative observation and analysis* (3rd ed.). Belmont, CA: Wadsworth.

Marshall, C., & Rossman, G. B. (1995). *Designing qualitative research* (2nd ed.). Thousand Oaks, CA: Sage.

Merton, R. K., Fiske, M., & Kendall, P. L. (1990). *The focused interview* (2nd ed.). New York: Free Press.

Merton, R. K., & Kendall, P. L. (1946). The focussed interview. *American Journal of Sociology, 51,* 541-557.

Morgan, D. L. (1989). Adjusting to widowhood: Do social networks really make it easier? *The Gerontologist, 29,* 101-107.

Morgan, D. L. (1996). Focus groups. In J. Hagan & K. S. Cook (Eds.), *Annual review of sociology* (Vol. 22, pp. 129-152). Palo Alto, CA: Annual Reviews.

Morgan, D. L. (1997). *Focus groups as qualitative research* (2nd ed.). Thousand Oaks, CA: Sage.

Morgan, D. L., & Spanish, M. T. (1984) Focus groups: A new tool for qualitative research. *Qualitative Sociology, 7,* 253-270.

O'Brien, K. J. (1993). Using focus groups to develop health surveys: An example from research on social relationships and AIDS-preventive behavior. In D. L. Morgan (Ed.), *Successful focus groups: Advancing the state of the art* (pp. 105-117). Thousand Oaks, CA: Sage.

Patton, M. Q. (1990). *Qualitative evaluation and research methods* (2nd ed.).Thousand Oaks, CA: Sage.

Stewart, D. W., & Shamdasani, P. N. (1990). *Focus groups: Theory and practice.* Thousand Oaks, CA: Sage.

Index to the Focus Group Kit

The letter preceding the page number refers to the volume, according to the following key:

G   Volume 1:   *The Focus Group Guidebook*
P   Volume 2:   *Planning Focus Groups*
Q   Volume 3:   *Developing Questions for Focus Groups*
M   Volume 4:   *Moderating Focus Groups*
I   Volume 5:   *Involving Community Members in Focus Groups*
A   Volume 6:   *Analyzing and Reporting Focus Group Results*

About the Author

David L. Morgan received his Ph.D. in sociology from the University of Michigan and did post-doctoral work at Indiana University. He is currently a professor in the Institute on Aging at Portland State University's College of Urban and Public Affairs. In addition to his continuing work with focus groups, he has a wide-ranging interest in research methods, including designs that combine qualitative and quantitative methods.  Within gerontology, his research interests center on the aging of the baby boomers—a topic that should keep him busy until his own retirement!